START YOUR ONLINE STORE

A STEP-BY-STEP GUIDE TO ESTABLISHING A
PROFITABLE ECOMMERCE BUSINESS WITH
SHOPIFY

SHOPIFY MADE EASY

BOOK 1

VERONICA JEANS

DISCLAIMER

Important Note on Shopify Changes:

Shopify updates its shopping platform frequently, and the information still applies if you see a different screen, window, or dashboard. I have tried staying current with the updates and updated as much as possible. I will publish ongoing Shopify updates on my website and in UPDATED books.

If you discover outdated information in this book, know an update is underway.

If you want updates, please sign up for my newsletter, which will also provide more information about Shopify, marketing, and what's new in the eCommerce and digital social media market, including new tools and apps -www.veronicajeans.com.

This book is written by Veronica Jeans and has no association with Shopify.

WEBSITE ADDRESSES IN THIS BOOK:

I have tried to make it easy for you to link to information, but if the link will not work, I created easy-to-read links with an accessible web address.

Disclaimer for the web addresses in this book may be affiliated links. We may receive a commission if you visit them and decide to buy something. This won't cost you any extra. We only include web addresses to products or services we use for our clients or would happily use ourselves.

INTRODUCTION

 "Products are made in the factory, but brands are created in the mind." – Walter Landor.

The purpose of writing this book is to assist entrepreneurs like you in establishing an online presence and initiating product sales with ease, without having to spend excessive time learning new skills.

This is **not** a guide on making millions through specific sales techniques or strategies. Instead, the focus is on setting up your **sales engine** effectively to **achieve successful product sales.**

Here is the secret to a successful business…

You need to learn from other people's experiences

You need to create a plan and goals and stay focused.

You need to follow the steps set out and not get distracted

You need a team.

And you need to be passionate about your product.

I will try to help you set up your business for success.

Through this book, I aim to share my experience with you, create a plan, and work together to complete the setup of your store, enabling you to start selling your products. We will work as a team and remain focused on achieving this goal. With this approach, your brand and store will hopefully showcase your passion for your products.

My Shopify books are designed to simplify the process of setting up your Shopify store, covering only the essentials required to get started. For additional information, I will refer you to my other books or tools.

In this particular book, I have incorporated my extensive experience in technology, business, financing, and eCommerce, both from my own business and clients, to provide you with an edge in your online venture.

The primary focus of this book is to help you **establish a memorable brand** and a **successful customer journey** that encourages visitors to return and purchase your products repeatedly.

With thousands of illustrations and links to helpful internet tools and apps, this authoritative guide provides a comprehensive blueprint for building a successful eCommerce business using Shopify, the leading eCommerce platform.

This book is not about the products you sell; instead, it concentrates on building a solid foundation for your business to ensure smooth operation and profitable product sales. By now, I assume you have a product or idea in mind for your online store.

WHAT MAKES THIS BOOK SPECIAL?

I update my books annually to keep up with the constant changes in Shopify. There is an abundance of information available on

Shopify's blogs, which can be overwhelming, making it difficult to set up and optimize your online business.

Setting up your Shopify store has never been easier with the step-by-step blueprint and screenshots provided in this book, allowing you to follow along without the need for technical expertise.

Using the methodology I teach my clients and students, I walk you through each step of setting up a Shopify store, drawing on my experience owning Shopify stores in the USA and internationally.

Each chapter of the book focuses on a specific subject or setting within the Shopify setup, accompanied by step-by-step instructions and screenshots of your Shopify dashboard, and includes numerous tips based on my experience assisting other Shopify owners in building their successful eCommerce businesses.

It is impossible to include all the necessary information in one book; therefore, this book focuses on the foundation of your ecommerce store.

This book is not about the setup of theme implementation, product uploading, social media channels and marketplaces like Amazon. To ensure your Shopify setup is not overwhelming, I have created the Shopify Made Easy book series, with each book taking you one step further in optimizing your Shopify store.

Shopify Made Easy series:

Book One

Start Your Online Business

A Step-by-Step Guide To Establishing a Profitable eCommerce Business with Shopify

Book Two

Build Your Shopify Brand

A Blueprint for Crafting Your Customer Journey to Maximize Sales

Book Three

Grow Your Shopify Business

A Comprehensive Guide to Boosting Your E-commerce Sales and Growing Your Business

See all my books on Amazon: https://veronicajeans.online/SME-series

HOW THIS BOOK WORKS

In this book, I will provide you with the location of each dashboard section in Shopify and guide you on the necessary steps to set up your store.

For further information, each chapter includes a reference section with links designed for easy comprehension, making them effortless to read and understand.

All the links are with my domain = *https://veronicajeans.online/ subject* instead of this very long confusing URL (browser link) example: [*https://app.ahrefs.com/site-audit/3401207/25/data-d0f4-11e7-8ed1-001e67ed4656&filterCollapsed=true*]

Throughout this book, I incorporate quotes from Shopify to provide additional verification for the steps you are executing, enhancing their reliability.

To ensure the accuracy of the information presented, I also include quotes from reliable sources.

All the images in this book are screenshots of the Shopify dashboard and have been optimized for printing. However, as website images, it is not possible to enhance them beyond what has been done for the book.

Once you have set up your Shopify store, this book will serve as an excellent reference, as it can be challenging to remember where all the settings are if you do not use them regularly. This book will simplify the process for you.

WHY SHOPIFY?

One question I am frequently asked is, "Do I need a website if I have a shopping cart?"

The answer is no; if you have a shopping platform like Shopify, you do not require a separate website. Shopify is an all-in-one shopping platform that includes your website, store, and blog, making it a complete web application for building and managing your online store.

One of the most significant advantages of Shopify is its user-friendliness. Even if you are not tech-savvy, you can easily set up your Shopify store without difficulty.

With Shopify, you get a website, store, and blog all in one package. If you register your domain with Shopify, you will also receive alias email addresses.

NOTE: Shopify is not a hosting email provider.

Shopify enables integration with various marketplaces and social media platforms, such as Facebook, Instagram, Amazon, eBay, Walmart, Pinterest, TikTok, Etsy, Raku, and many others, continually expanding its reach.

With Shopify, you can directly integrate with other vendors to source, dropship, or print-on-demand products from China, Europe, and the United States.

Setting up payment options in Shopify is easy and convenient, with built-in payment systems that allow you to set up your payment merchant account by simply adding your information to the Shopify admin. Additionally, Shopify permits the acceptance of multiple currencies, making it a genuinely international shopping cart with several payment options.

Order processing and shipping can be conveniently managed within your Shopify admin, where you can generate shipping labels, invoices, tracking, and more with ease.

While Shopify can host your domain name, you also have the option to use a domain name hosted by a third-party provider. If you have your domain name with a third-party hosting company, you can connect it to your Shopify store.

Why would you register your domain with Shopify and not with a third-party domain host?

·   *It's easy to use and has many features that can help you grow your business.*

·   *Shopify hosts it, so you don't need to worry about setting up and maintaining your website server.*

·   *It's a hosted platform that can be accessed and managed from anywhere worldwide.*

·   *It comes with SSL encryption (HTTPS), so you don't have to set that up separately*

·   *You get privacy protection for free from Shopify.*

As a guide to all of my books, I have developed a free bonus course that provides downloadable worksheets, bonus video content, and access to all the resources and links referenced in this book.

Here is a link to my RESOURCES & TOOLS page:

https://veronicajeans.online/resources

Bonus tool: There is also my onboarding worksheet that you can use to add all your store, social, and password information.

TECHNOLOGY

What technological requirements do you need before starting your online store?

To ensure that your product images appear great, you may need a laptop or computer to bulk upload your products. It is recommended that you have a laptop with at least 16GB of memory, as it will make it easier to create images and videos, and bulk upload.

You have the option of running your store from a mobile device or an iPad/similar device using the Shopify App, but it is recommended to use a laptop or desktop computer to add products and information efficiently.

You can connect to a regular printer or label printer to print shipping labels and invoices as needed.

CONTENTS

CHAPTER 1
CREATE YOUR SHOPIFY STORE FOUNDATION

BEFORE YOU REGISTER your Shopify store, there are important business decisions you need to make. In this chapter, you will set up your business foundation so your Shopify setup is easy, without any delays or frustrations.

WHAT THIS BOOK WILL NOT DO

- *Help you find products.*
- *Find drop shipping or manufacturing companies.*
- *Provide Information about a Pro Point of Sale (POS) system and hardware setup.*

What to Expect in This Chapter:

- *The Difference Between a Shopping Platform and a Cart*
- *The Right Way to Set Up Shopify*
- *10 Things to Prepare Before You Start*
- *Find Your Unique Domain and Store Name*
- *Start Your Shopify Store*

THE DIFFERENCE BETWEEN A SHOPPING PLATFORM AND A SHOPPING CART

Shopping cart software is a piece of e-commerce software on a web server that allows visitors to an Internet site to select items for eventual purchase.

Wikipedia says:

> *"The software allows online shopping customers to accumulate a list of items for purchase. At the point of sale, the software typically calculates a total for the order, including freight transport, postage, packaging, and labeling. The software computes associated taxes as applicable."*

Shopify says:

> *"A shopping platform, or more accurately, an e-commerce platform is a piece of online subscription software that allows you to build an online business. It gives you all the tools to create and manage your site, including products and day-to-day operations.*
>
> *Shopify is a subscription software service that offers you to create a website and use its shopping cart solution to sell, ship, and manage your products.*
>
> *Using their service, you can access an easy-to-use admin panel where you can add products, process orders, and enter store data.*
>
> *Shopify is a complete commerce platform that lets you start, grow, and manage a business. Create and customize an online store. Sell in multiple places, including web, mobile, social media, online marketplaces, brick-and-mortar*

locations, and pop-up shops. Manage products, inventory, payments, and shipping."

THE RIGHT WAY TO SET UP SHOPIFY

I know you want to immediately upload your products and return to all the less important stuff to set up your store later. If you follow my Shopify setup methodology, you will have fewer frustrations and you will know you have set up your online business for success.

Start with the business basics first before you get to the fun stuff.

I will give you some tasks to do before you even start on Shopify. These are essential steps, not to be ignored. We will set up your theme after you create your foundation for your store. If you create the foundation before implementing all the options in your Shopify theme, like collections, products, pages, etc., your store will be set up for faster growth.

10 THINGS TO PREPARE BEFORE YOU START

Before you launch your Shopify store, here are 10 things to prepare before you start your Shopify store.

1. Research and register your brand and domain name with Shopify - more information in this chapter.

2. Register your company as an entity or DBA (Doing Business As). Consult with an accountant about the tax benefits of owning an entity instead of being an individual. Research the information about what you can legally do in your state or country. Advice from Matt Beaudoin, the owner of Mystic Knotwork during an interview:

"Well, Deepak Chopra talks about living your life backward. Know where you want to end up and then work towards that end. The big thing to do again was to LLC yourself. Get your documents in order first because they're not expensive. I had a really, really, really painful year when I got to send the IRS 120% of my take-home pay in taxes. Only to get it all back in April because I was double taxing myself - I waited way too long. So both my personal entity and my LLC were paying taxes simultaneously. So taking that step when it's small, and it's not much to do, you get those in order."

3. Get a sales tax permit. Apply for your particular state or country. If you sell any products, you must collect sales tax. Each state is different, so check the information on your state business websites. Even if you are doing business as an individual, you will still need a sales tax permit.

4. Open a business bank account. I know it is easy to use a personal bank account, but it can get very messy quickly. You need to keep your personal expenses apart from your business expenses. You will be collecting sales tax. It is a great idea to keep that sales tax revenue separate from your business revenue because it is not your money. Again, consult with a tax consultant about what you can and cannot do.

5. Know what you want to sell. Start your business with a clear path and goals of what you will sell and where you will sell it. This book is not about sourcing products; it is about creating a successful and profitable customer journey.

6. Know the details of how you, your manufacturer, or drop shipper will fulfill your products. You need to be clear about how you will ship your products and what it entails to ship products. I cover many details and tips about shipping in chapter 8 but do your own research as well.

7. Migrating your store. If you are migrating your store from another system to Shopify, ensure you have the CSV files for your products, customers, orders, etc., ready to import. Migrating information is not always a smooth path, but there are great apps that can help in this endeavor.

8. Know your brand. Your brand is the difference between you and your competition. It's what makes a lasting impression on customers and convinces them to buy from you. In this instance, you will need a logo, brand colors, and ideas of what your website will look like to launch your Shopify theme.

9. Use my brand list. There is more to business than just branding. I have a full checklist available for all the aspects of what you need to set up for your business, from business cards to post boxes and everything in between. Check out the link to my resource list at the end of this chapter.

10. Create a business information checklist. This is a list of all your online accounts like Shopify, Facebook, Google, etc., and contact information, email addresses, etc. I have a free business information worksheet available to copy and use. Here you can add all the information you need to collect, but it is also a great record of all your accounts and login information.

FIND YOUR UNIQUE DOMAIN AND STORE NAME

Bottom line: People should understand your brand name even when you say it in a noisy, crowded bar.

Step 1. Research before you decide to choose a brand name.

How do you choose a brand name? Choosing a brand name is very emotional for most entrepreneurs. We tend to choose cute names or something connected to our lives or events.

A memorable name can strengthen our brand and create an emotional connection to our customers.

If you think of a big brand name, like Coca-Cola, you think of cuddly Christmas bears, right?

Thanks to Harvard's implicit association test, we now understand that our brains quickly draw threads between words and emotions. According to a test by Customer Thermometer, 65% of US consumers have an emotional attachment to their favorite brands.

Your brand name will play a big role in your brand's marketing success. It has a few criteria:

1. Easy to remember - (you have half a second to be remembered)

2. Availability - Search for your dot com name and see if it is available. If it is not available, do not choose another domain extension. **The most commonly searched extension is .com.** People remember "Dotcom" most easily. Step 2 will go into detail about pitfalls with domain names.

3. Keep it short - Using long, overly complex domain names also increases the risk of typos or misspellings. For example, themissingpiecepuzzlecompany.com & parisianspurein dulgence.com have both shortened their domain name to themissingpiecepuzzle.com and parisianspure.com. Since you also need to create a business email address, simplicity is important. Keep it short and sweet by using just one or two words. Sometimes it does not work as with the puzzle company, but she could not shorten it too much because then she loses her keywords in her domain name.

4. Easy to spell - Typos happen. While you can't control the occasional fat-finger mishap, you can minimize confusion on exactly what people should be typing when pulling up your site. BoneLock.com is easy to remember and spell, Invicible.com is not and is most often misspelled as Invisible.com - which Invisalign owns. If misspelled when searching for your domain or store, at least it is not competition.

5. Sound out the name aloud - mysticknotwork.com has two interpretations. Make sure it does not have rude connotations unless that is what you are going for. Mystic Knotwork was probably not going for that.

6. Don't be too niche or trendy - Fads and buzzwords disappear very quickly, so keep your name evergreen.

7. Be descriptive - Consider what your store sells and give it a more descriptive name. When you use a more descriptive name, the chances of popping up when people are searching are higher than if you have a 'cutesy' name.

8. You can also use your own name, play around with it, or shorten it for simplicity, especially for fashion or skincare. Here are some examples, Veronica Beard Jeans is veronicabeard.com, Tata Harper is tataharper.com, although she has also added tataharperskincare.com because she sells skincare. Even though my name is closely associated with Veronica Beard's Jeans, I am on the #1 page on Google. I show you my secret in my 'Content Marketing ECommerce Secrets - How to compete with big brands to be #1.'

9. Do not choose a name that is similar to a larger brand - Check the domain and business name for trademarks. You don't want to get into any legal issues. This confuses people because they remember the big brand, and you are open to being prosecuted. My sons decided to create an eCommerce store. Paintzilla.com, and we did get a lawyer's letter from the company Godzilla from Japan to cease and desist. There is a wealth of information online on deciding what to choose for your domain name. I encourage you to do as much research as possible.

> Pro Tip: Use Tools - Business Name Generator - https://www.squadhelp.com/business-name-generator
>
> Use domain generators to find different variations for your name. Here is one: https://instantdomainsearch.com/domain/generator/

Step 2. Check your preferred domain's availability.

You can use 'whois.org' to find out. Type in your chosen name and check if it is available. (**https://whois.org**/). You can try this on Shopify.

[1.1.1]

Avoid a hyphen or double letters because nobody remembers them. If you were to use the same domain name as a competitor with a different extension, your customers are likely to go to the .com. Voila, your competitor has new customers thanks to you. If you register a .net or any other extension, you might miss out on potential customers. For example, I wanted to register one of my Shopify stores with the domain name 'Kalahari.com.' Unfortunately, Kalahari was available but not with the .com extension.

If you are local to, for instance, Australia, you might choose the .au extension.

Here is the kicker, you do not know who will own the .com extension in the future. So, it could affect your business adversely. Double-check that the domain is not closely related to (or, horrors, owned by) an inappropriate adult site. This scenario has seriously unwanted complications!

MOST IMPORTANT!

If somebody else already owns the domain name you have chosen, do some research to see who owns the domain name and what they are selling. You might be able to buy the domain name for a fee. It might be worth it if it is precisely the name you want.

Step 3. Choose several names!

Don't get married to the name. If you cannot find the perfect name right now, choose whatever is the best and know that you can always rebrand. So many companies do a rebrand for various reasons, and one of the main advantages is that it makes the brand look fresh and in sync with their customers' expectations.

> Pro Tip: Register different domain names. As an example, I registered Kalaharigold.com and Kalaharioil.com.

It is all about controlling your brand name and making it as difficult as possible for competitors or spammers to home in on your customers.

Also, register the plural of your domain name.

Many years ago, a client of mine had a domain name with the product in singular form. To set the scene - The family business was 30 years old, and he was excited to get online. He manufactured flags and flagpoles and all the accessories. He also installed the flagpoles locally.

A competitor registered his domain name with the product in plural form. He had hardly any overhead because he was a solopreneur doing business from home. He easily became a major competitor to my client.

This is an example of what can happen if you do not register all of your logical domain names in different variations. You do not have to go overboard but register the domain names that will directly affect you. Use the tools I suggested in the resources. This makes it easy to get ideas and variations of your favorite name.

START YOUR SHOPIFY STORE

**Where to find? https://Shopify.com*

Step 1. Register your Shopify store.

Now that you have decided what your store and brand name will be, start your Shopify store. Start the registration process for your new store with this link: **Shopify.com**

This link will take you straight to the Shopify website to register your store.

[1.1.4]

Add your email to the registration prompts. The email name can be a permanent email address for your store. You can change it once your store is set up.

Choose either of the next options - you are just starting or are selling online.

shopify

Let's get started. Which of these best describes you?
We'll help you get set up based on your business needs.

I'm just starting   I'm already selling online or in person

[1.1.4a]

You do not need a business email to register your Shopify store. The email registered here is your email address to access your Shopify store admin.

This email will also be registered as your email for communicating with your Shopify store.

In the next chapter, I will show you how to change your email address for communication with Shopify and explain the reasons why you should have a business email address.

> Pro Tip: Do save your password - although, if you do not remember your password, you can create a new password when you log in the next time.

Next, choose all options - Where would you like to sell?

- *Online store - if your online store is not checked, your products will not be available online.*
- *Social Media - This option is an important part of your marketing efforts.*
- *In-Person - If you are going to sell at events, retail stores, or pop-ups. If you are not sure you can always add this app later.*
- *An existing website or blog - This will add a Buy Button option to your store. These you can use in blogs, newsletters, other websites, etc. This app is very handy.*
- *Online marketplaces.*
- *I'm not sure - if you choose this option, you can still add all the other apps in your store after you set up your Shopify store. It just makes it easier for set up to check all the previous options and you can always delete any if you are not going to use them.*

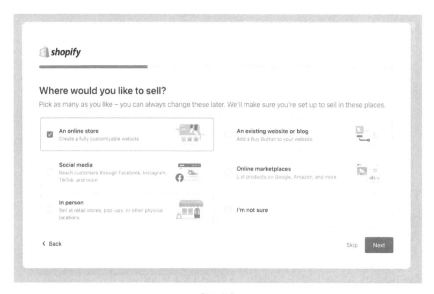

[1.1.4b]

Next, choose the social media channels you want to market your products to - you can add them later, but it makes it easier to check them at this stage. You do not have to use them even if you checked them here.

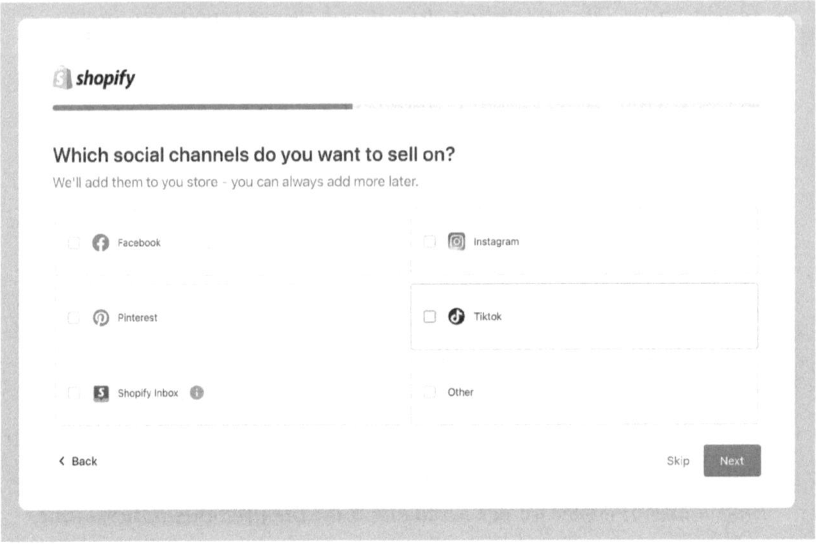

[1.1.4c]

Next, which marketplaces do you want to sell to:

- *Google*
- *Etsy*
- *Amazon*
- *eBay*
- *Other*

The only marketplace apps that will be implemented immediately in your Shopify store are the free Shopify apps. Google. Etsy, Amazon, and eBay are all paid marketplace apps you can add to your store. You have a choice of apps to implement. These are created by third-party Shopify vendors. I cover all the different marketplace implementations in my book - Optimize Your Shopify store.

[1.1.4d]

Next, do you have an online audience or a following:

If you answer no, then you will be pushed to the next question. If you choose yes, there will be a lot of options to choose from, but as I mentioned before, not all the social media apps will be added.

[1.1.4e]

In this case, only Facebook, Instagram, TikTok, and Pinterest apps will be added to your store. All the other social media channels are paid Shopify apps, which are created by third-party Shopify vendors.

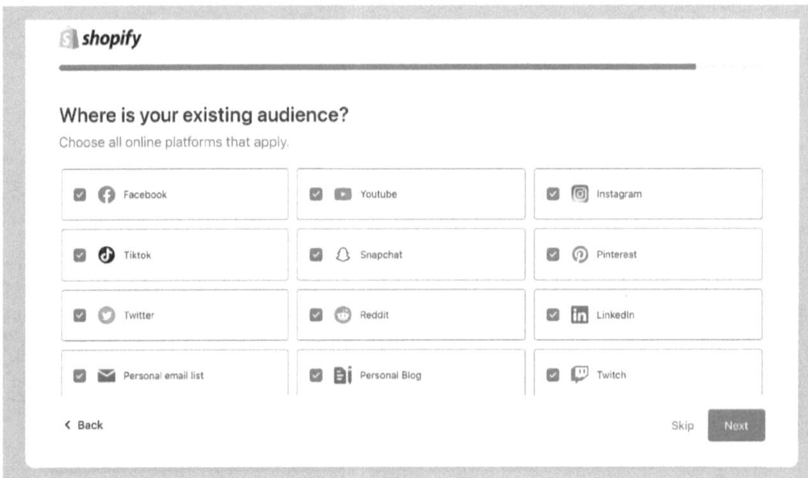

[1.1.4f]

In the following image you can see some more choices for you.

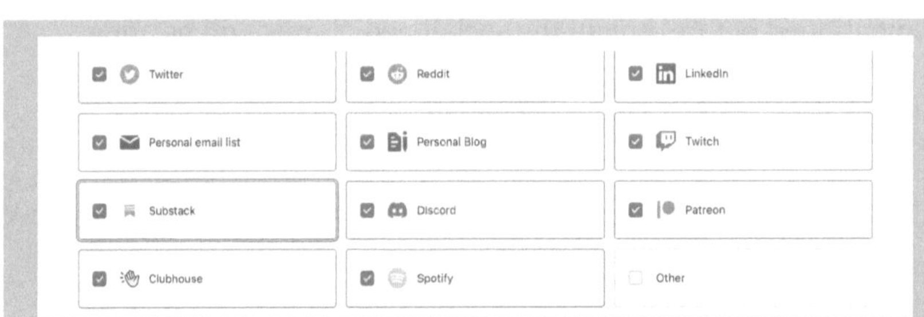

[1.1.4g]

Next, you will add your store name.

When you add your store name to the registration page, this is your Shopify store admin name. It will look like this:

https://kalaharigold-com.myshopify.com/admin

This is a temporary URL to start setting up your Shopify store. Once you set up your store, you can choose to keep it as is or replace it with a custom domain name.

You can use this as your Shopify store name, but this is a **sub-domain** of the Shopify domain name. In essence, this is a Shopify brand name and not yours. You need to register your own brand domain name for customers to remember your brand, e.g. KalahariGold.com

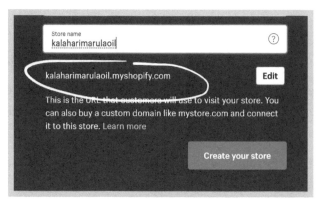

[1.1.4j]

Shopify will let you know if your domain is not available. **The domain names that are verified in this section are available worldwide.** You can see that Shopify will add a number to the domain name if there is another Shopify store with the same store name.

As you see in the following image that the brand name has a number because I have previously already registered the Shopify store with the domain name Kalaharigold.

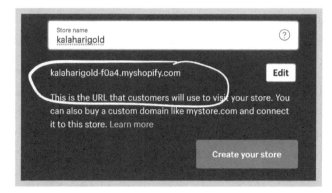

[1.1.4i]

This is a good indicator that your domain name is not available.

You **can** edit the suggested Shopify domain name. Make it easy to remember because this is how you will log in to your Shopify admin dashboard for your store.

Here is another example of a new store name. As you can see in the following image, Kalaharimarulaoil is available.

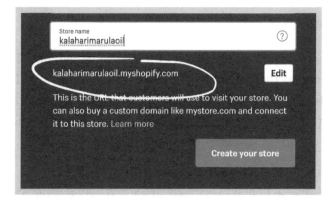

[1.1.4j]

Remember, this does not mean your domain name is registered on the world wide web (internet). To own your domain name, it must be registered with a domain name registrar. We are lucky that

Shopify is now a domain name registrar, and you can register your domain name with Shopify.

IF you choose to migrate your Shopify store, no apps are added to your store to help with the migration.

[1.1.4k]

The best app I have used for migrating a store to Shopify is called 'Matrixify.' Get it from the Shopify App Store. Or it would be best to hire an expert. 'Matrixify' will also support DFY (done for you) migrations. More about migrating your store in Book 2, chapter 4.

Step 2. Wait for your store to be set up!

You need to wait for Shopify to set up and add the information you have added. Now your Shopify store will be created while this image displays.

[1.1.6]

Step 3. The first look at your Shopify store

The following image is one example of the home page on your dashboard. This might vary a little bit depending on the options you checked. But it will be similar.

[1.1.7]

SET UP YOUR SHOPIFY STORE

You can follow the Shopify setup suggestions on your dashboard's home page, but I will show you how to set it up the easy way.

The system in all of my books is how I set up all my clients' Shopify stores. I will show you how to navigate best to ensure your store has all the capabilities to have a successfully functioning store.

Each chapter will cover different settings and options in your Shopify store. Some of the content is divided into different chapters due to the many options in a section.

The following images show the Shopify dashboard's home page and the dashboard's main sections.

[1.1.7a]

Each main section will give you more options to add or find more information.

I will show you step-by-step how to add the information you need for your Shopify store.

There is a detailed legend for each chapter's content, indicating what steps and details are covered.

Each section in Shopify will be indicated as follows so you know exactly where everything is located:

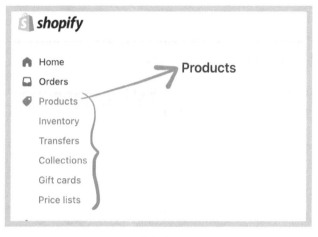

[1.1.7b]

Once you know where you are, I will take you step-by-step through the whole section.

If I have tools or resources to assist you, all the links will be at the end of each chapter.

And after each chapter, you will get a Quick Action Checklist to ensure you have all the steps suggested in the chapter, at a glance.

WHERE DO WE START?

As we have researched the brand name in this chapter, we will start with claiming your domain name in the next chapter.

NOTE: We are not following the sections in Settings as set out in your dashboard. Since we have done our due diligence in this chapter about domain names, we will start with claiming your domain name and setting up your business emails.

I strongly suggest following my methodology in setting up your Shopify store.

. . .

RESOURCES:

A branding ideas list is available online on my website - *https://veronicajeans.online/resources*

The business information worksheet/checklist is on the resources page.

https://veronicajeans.online/resources

Use Tools - (https://www.squadhelp.com/business-name-generator)

Use domain generators to find different variations for your name - here is one - **https://instantdomainsearch.com/domain/generator/**

The best app I have used for migrating a store to Shopify is called "Matrixify." Get it from the Shopify App Store.

Link to Matt's interview -https://veronicajeans.-com/blogs/virtual-eCommerce-summit-2020/matt-beaudoin

CHAPTER 2
SHOPIFY DOMAINS & EMAILS

YOU HAVE STARTED your Shopify store and registered your brand name for your Shopify store. In Chapter 1, you researched your domain name and availability. Now we will claim the domain name for your brand. Once you have claimed your brand domain name, you can create some business email addresses.

COMMONLY USED WORDS

First, here are some quick explanations about commonly used words in this chapter.

What is a domain name?

Shopify says: *"A domain is a URL, or the website address, where your customers go to find your store online."*

A domain name is an address you type into a website browser address bar to get to a website. For example, Google is https://google.com. My domain name is https://veronicajeans.com. A domain name is unique to your website and cannot be shared between different websites.

What is a hosting company?

A hosting company is a company you can use to register your domain name. You register your domain name with one of the larger hosting companies like 'GoDaddy.com,' 'Name.com,' 'Bluehost.com,' or Shopify. Registering your domain name with Shopify is the easiest, no-hassle option because you do not know how to change your DNS or other domain name registration information.

What is a Top-Level Domain?

A top-level domain is the extension of your domain name, either .com, .net. or .org. Country top-level domains consist of 2 letters for the country, for instance, .au for Australia. There are several others, and new ones are being created all the time. The most searched for TLD is .com. TLDs help customers find your business easily online. Dot com is the TLD that people remember most easily.

What to Expect in This Chapter:

- *Register Your Domain in Shopify*
- *Claim Your Domain Name in Shopify*
- *Connect Your Existing Domain Name in Shopify*
- *Transfer Your Domain to Shopify*
- *Create Your Email Addresses*

REGISTER YOUR DOMAIN IN SHOPIFY

Where to find this in Shopify? Online Store > Settings > Domains

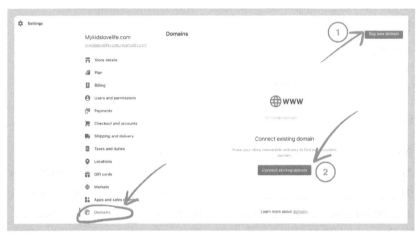

[1.2.1]

When you register your domain name, the registration cost is a once-a-year cost. Your host, in this case, Shopify, will let you know when you need to pay for your yearly domain name renewal.

There are 2 choices to register your domain in Shopify.

- *Register your domain name with Shopify. When you have not registered your domain name, Shopify will be your domain host for your domain name.*
- *Connect your domain name with Shopify. If your domain name is registered with a third-party domain host, then this is how to connect your domain name with your Shopify store.*

CLAIM YOUR DOMAIN NAME IN SHOPIFY

***Where to find this in Shopify? Settings > Domains**

The easiest way to claim your domain name is to register your domain name in Shopify.

Step 1. Add Preferred Domain Name

Add your preferred domain name. A buy button will appear if you have done your due diligence to ensure your domain name is available.

[1.2.2]

Step 2. Buy Your Domain Name

Add your credit card information to your Shopify account, which will be used for all purchases and bills in Shopify. For instance, the cost for the domain name (yearly), Shopify subscription plan (monthly or yearly), and Shopify Apps (monthly or yearly).

[1.2.3]

The next choice is whether you want to **auto-renew** your domain name registration every year. I would strongly suggest checking the option. The subscription for your domain name is a yearly charge and it is easy to forget.

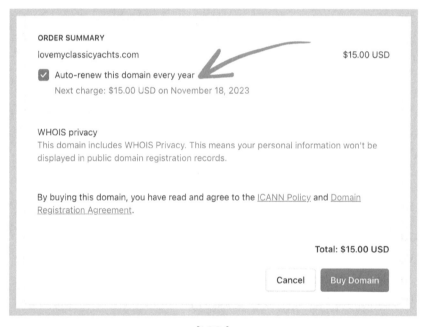

[1.2.3a]

I lost my domain name veronicaleejeans.com because I did not have it on renewal. I was lucky none of the domain brokers did not snatch it. I would have to pay fees to the broker etc. This can happen to anybody. Losing your brand name can have major consequences.

'Primary Domain' is the domain name visible to the internet. Your domain name will appear in the browser window to your visitors when they visit your website.

[1.2.18]

Step 3. Add More Domain Names to Shopify

Both Shopify-managed domains and third-party-hosted domains can be connected to your Shopify store. However, only one of the domain names can be your primary domain. The rest of the domains names are forwarded to the 'Primary Domain'. If a visitor enters the second domain name (which does not have to be the same as your primary domain name) in the browser, they will be forwarded to your primary domain name.

For example, 'eCommerceplanner.com' forwards to 'veronicajeans.com.'

As you can see, I have several domains that point or forward to my primary domain name. Why would I do this? For instance, I have a domain name for my book, and if I have that link anywhere, it will show my website.

Can you add more domain names to Shopify?

If you are adding more domain names, repeat the action and add your domain name to the text box.

You can have 20 domains attached to your Shopify store.

Why would you do that?

I have a domain name for each of my books and courses, i.e. shopifyoptimizeyourstore.com, and eCommercesuccess.com. Each of these domain names is attached to my veronicajeans.com Shopify store.

[1.2.18]

Step 4. Add Sub-Domain

Hubspot.com says, *"The most common subdomain is www, which stands for World Wide Web. This subdomain contains a website's homepage and its most important pages. The www subdomain is so widely used that most domain registrars include it with domain name purchases."*

Examples of why you would set up a sub-domain:

If you have a WordPress, Squarespace, etc., website and do not want to change your website but only want to add a store, you can set up a sub-domain. The sub-domain would be your store website address.

If you have a Shopify Store Plus account, you can add a wholesale sub-domain with a completely different homepage.

I have added a few sub-domains so you can see what it looks like in the following image.

[1.2.25]

What happens if you add a sub-domain?

A subdomain is a separate website with its own unique content, design, and domain name. It is not part of your main website.

If you use a subdomain for Shopify, your Shopify store will be hosted on that subdomain and will not be connected to your main website.

Visitors to your main website will not be able to access your Shopify store unless they know the address of your subdomain.

You will need to promote your Shopify store separately from your main website.

[1.2.26]

CONNECT YOUR EXISTING DOMAIN NAME IN SHOPIFY

Where to find this in Shopify? Settings > Domains

This is about when your domain in Shopify.

Step 1. Connect your existing domain. Name

Click on 'Connect Existing Domain' as shown below. Next, add your preferred domain name and go to the next instructions.

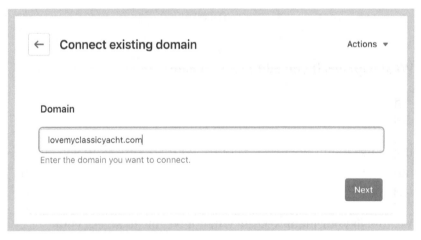

[1.2.4]

If your domain name is not claimed, Shopify will indicate that your domain name is available for purchase. Click on the Buy domain, and you will claim your domain name.

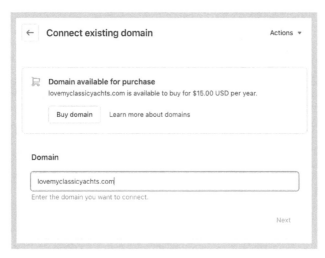

1.2.5a]

Step 2. Connect your hosting company

If your domain is registered with a Shopify-partnered hosting company, your hosting company name will appear. See the following image to see what happens.

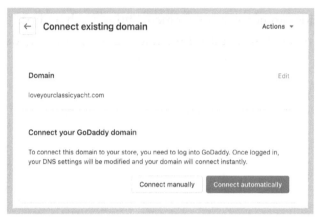

[1.2.5]

You have 2 choices:

1. Connect Automatically

2. Connect Manually

Your first inclination is to click the highlighted button - Connect automatically, which is the best option.

Step 3. Connect Automatically

Your Shopify-partnered hosting company will automatically connect your domain name to Shopify and create all the appropriate DNS (domain name server) entries.

You might have to add your DNS (Domain Name Server) information to your domain host dashboard so you can verify your domain.

[1.2.6]

Even though you choose to connect automatically, you will still have to add the details to your DNS in your domain host dashboard.

In the following image, you can see that Shopify provides you with the details of what you need to add to connect your domain automatically to Shopify.

The changes or additions are:

A Record = 23.337.38.65

CNAME = shops.myshopify.com (shops is the store name you registered in the beginning when you started in Shopify)

Connecting your domain

A and CNAME entered incorrectly

Check that you've entered the required values, and verify your connection again.

A RECORD ⓘ

Name: @ Copy
Current IP address: 34.102.136.180
Required value: **23.227.38.65** Copy

CNAME ⓘ

Name: **www** Copy
Current value: **loveyourclassicyacht.com**
Required value: **shops.myshopify.com** Copy

⚠ **Domain connection incomplete**
Some providers take a few minutes to update settings. You can check later for connection updates, or you can try again.

Add domain

Follow the step-by-step instructions and verify your connection again.   Verify connection

[1.2.7]

Once you have added the details to your DNS in your domain host, you will wait 30 minutes to 24 hours, depending on your host, before your Shopify store will connect to the domain name.

Go to step 5 to see how to add the details.

Step 4. Connect manually

If you are not automatically connected to Shopify by your hosting provider when prompted, follow the instructions Shopify provides or get an expert to help.

Your hosting provider support should be proficient in adding the information to your domain.

Add your preferred brand name to the domain registration section. Shopify will automatically let you know if somebody else owns the domain.

Step 5. Add information to the DNS

Normally the information is under 'Manage Your DNS.'

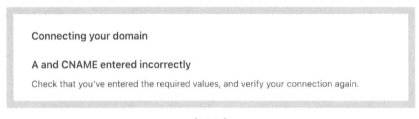

Connecting your domain

A and CNAME entered incorrectly

Check that you've entered the required values, and verify your connection again.

[1.2.7a]

Find the DNS settings or domain management area. Change the following records: Point the **A** record to the Shopify IP address 23.227.38.65. If necessary, change the **Host** name to the @ symbol. Delete any other A records on the domain if there are any present. Point the **CNAME** record with name **www** to shops. myshopify.com.

The following image shows the A record:

[1.2.8]

The following image shows the CNAME record:

[1.2.9]

Once you have completed all the steps, your domain name will appear in Shopify domain settings as follows:

It will show you who is hosting your domain name as well in the domain name information.

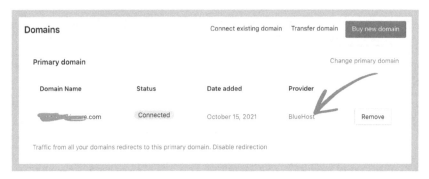

[1.2.19]

Step 6. Domain name privacy

This provides privacy of the information attached to your domain name.

[1.2.12]

Wikepedia.org says: *"Domain privacy (often called Whois privacy) is a service offered by a number of domain name registrars.[1] A user buys privacy from the company, who in turn replaces the user's information in the WHOIS with the information of a forwarding service (for email and sometimes postal mail, it is done by a proxy server)."*

If you don't want SPAM, you will need domain name privacy.

> Pro Tip: Register additional singular or plural versions of your domain name, including a couple of variations. You want to ensure your competition will not grab a similar domain name and with that your traffic and customers to your store.

For Example:

Singular - themissingpiecepuzzle.com.

Plural - themissingpiecepuzzles.com

Variations - missingpuzzlepiece.com etc.

TRANSFER YOUR DOMAIN TO SHOPIFY

Where to find this in Shopify? Settings > Domains

There are a few details to know before you initiate a transfer:

- *You need to own the domain name which means you registered the domain name and are paying a yearly subscription for the domain name.*
- *Know who your domain name host is, what your login information is and your email address for communication.*
- *The email address you use for communication must not belong to the domain that you are transferring. You are changing domain name hosts and your email address is attached to your domain name.*

- *Shopify does not provide email hosting. You will need a third-party email hosting company for your domain/ brand? name email addresses. Shopify will forward email alias addresses.*
- *When you transfer your domain to Shopify, you pay the yearly fee for your domain name. A new domain host is registering your domain with Internet Corporation for Assigned Names and Numbers (ICANN) (ICANN coordinates these unique domain names across the world.)*

Step 1. Check eligibility for transfer

First, review your domain provider's transfer policy.

You can check whether your domain is eligible for transfer from your Shopify admin. Some domains, such as .ca and .co. or uk domains, aren't eligible for transfer.

Step 2. Add your domain name

Enter the domain you would like to transfer.

Transfer domain

Domain

ecommercesuccessplanner.com

Enter the domain you would like to transfer to Shopify

Next

Or you can connect your domain to Shopify (management will remain with your current registrar).

[1.2.20]

NOTE: Sometimes your domain cannot be transferred, as it has been transferred or registered within the last 60 days. You will have to wait the for the 60 days to expire and try again.

Step 3. Verify your domain name

You need to complete these steps with your current provider:

- *Unlock your domain.*
- *Get an authorization code from your provider.*

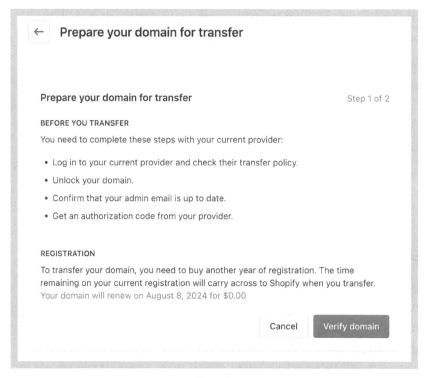

[1.2.21]

Pro Tip: Contact your domain host to help with this transition. Each one will have the information in a different area. Most third-party domain hosts' customer service representatives are very helpful.

Once you have unlocked your domain and you have the authorization codes, you can continue with the transfer of your domain.

Step 4. Add the authorization codes

When prompted by Shopify, pay for your yearly domain name subscription.

NOTE: It can take up to 20 days to transfer your domain. Your domain continues working during the transfer process. Although, some registrars will transfer your domain in the same day.

The following image shows how your domain name will appear in Shopify once the transfer is complete.

ⓚ **ecommercesuccessplanner.com** Redirects to veronicajeans.com	Online Store

[1.2.22]

DIFFERENT EMAIL NOMENCLATURE

Not many people understand the differences because the language used for each email option has been simplified. I have added the following explanation of different types of email options to understand what you need when you have a business and an online store. An email program differs from an email service, an email account, or even an email address.

EMAIL HOSTING COMPANY: Namecheap.com says: *"Email hosting is a service in which a hosting provider rents out email servers to its users. While free versions are available with many hosting companies, many businesses take advantage of the flexibility and power of professional email services. Professional email hosting occurs when incoming and outgoing emails are managed by a separate shared or dedicated mail server."*

EMAIL PROGRAM: Software in the user's computer, tablet or smartphone that provides the ability to send and receive email messages and file attachments.

EMAIL SERVICE: An email service is something like Outlook.com, Yahoo! Mail, or Gmail, or the services provided by your ISP, domain hosting company, school, or place of employment. Their service includes the software or program that sends and receives your email messages. Think of it as an apartment building where you live.

This is also an email provider that hosts your domain email addresses and provides the email service that stores all your email information.

EMAIL ACCOUNT: An email account is a relationship you establish with an email service and all the storage, features, and functionality included. This may consist of more than email services. For example, Microsoft and Gmail accounts have email and cloud storage services, messaging services, calendaring, contacts, and much more. An account is often, though not always, identified by a single email address. This is still the apartment building where you live.

EMAIL ADDRESS: An email address uniquely identifies your mailbox provided by your email service. When a message is sent to your email address, it's collected by your email service and placed in a mailbox, which you access through your email account. Email addresses are always in this format: name@domain.extension. Your email account is your apartment. Your email address is like the apartment number.

We tend to call our email addresses and email messages the same. So, you'd ask somebody for their email (which is their email address) and receive an email (email message) from somebody. That is where confusion occurs.

I know this might be confusing and you will probably not need to know the details, but it will make sense when we start setting up your business and alias email addresses.

Where are your business or domain email addresses hosted?

Your business or domain email addresses are hosted with a third-party email provider.

The following image shows the relationship between all the services, hosting companies, where they live, and what they do.

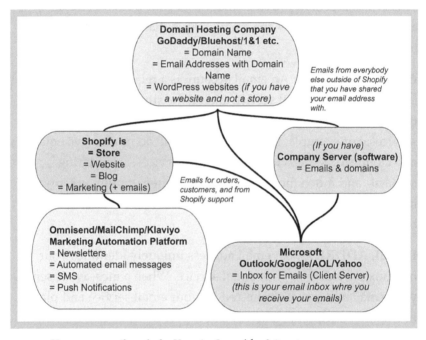

How your email works by Veronica Jeans (check it out on my resources page)

Shopify does not host your emails, even if you register your domain in Shopify. Therefore, your best option is to get a third-party email hosting company for your business emails.

Shopify can, however, provide you with forwarding or alias emails that correspond to your registered domain name.

As you can see in the following image, my business email is hello@ veronicajeans.com which forwards to my veronica.jeans@ gmail.com account.

[1.2.23]

CREATE YOUR EMAIL ADDRESSES

When you register your domain from a third-party hosting company, you need to create your business, forwarding, or alias email addresses with your hosting company

Shopify says: *"Shopify doesn't provide email hosting, but if you buy a domain through Shopify, or transfer your domain to Shopify, then you can set up an unlimited number of forwarding (alias) email addresses (for example, info@johnsapparel.com) for free.*

You will need to use a third-party email hosting service if you want to send an email from your custom domain forwarding address. For example, if you are using Zoho Mail or G Suite, you can connect the hosting service

to your domain in Shopify. If you're using another hosting email service, you can add an MX Record to connect the email address to your domain by editing your DNS settings."

When you have added your domain name, Shopify will show you how to add a third-party email host.

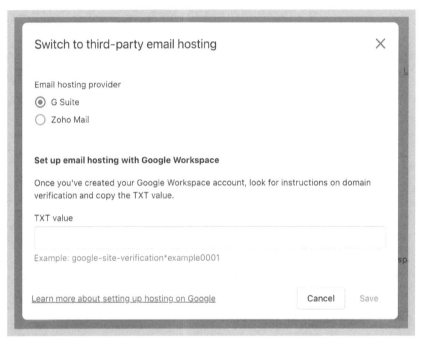

[1.2.24]

Can you use your personal email?

It looks more professional and trustworthy to have a company email address. But you can use a personal email.

Shopify will provide you with an email alias address with your domain name and then forward it to your personal email address.

YOUR BUSINESS EMAILS FOR YOUR SHOPIFY STORE

Where to find this? Shopify > Online store > Domains

Create three types of emails for your Shopify store.

- ***Method 1.*** *Email Alias Forwarding to Your External Email Address in Shopify.*
- ***Method 2.*** *Email address in a third-party email provider connected to Shopify - G-suite or Zoho.*
- ***Method 3.*** *Email address in a third-party email provider - for example, GoDaddy.*

Method 1. Email Alias Forwarding to Your External Email Address in Shopify

Setting up your emails with Zoho or G-Suite is straightforward. They have a user-friendly interface, and all you have to do is follow the prompts. Click on the domain name where you want to add an email address.

[1.2.23]

Step 1. Manage your domain.

Set up your alias or forward emails for the existing domain you registered and paid for in Shopify.

Once you click on 'Manage,' you can manage your domain and email forwarding addresses, transfers of domains, etc.

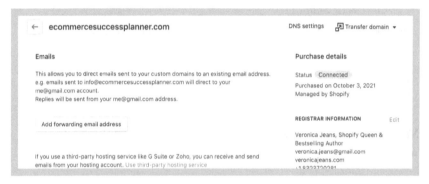

[1.2.27]

Step 2. Add the alias or forwarding email addresses.

Add any alias email addresses you want. Ensure the emails will be sent to a verified email address to which you have access.

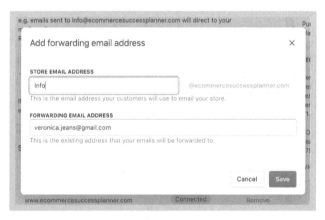

[.1.2.28]

Step 3. Verify the email address

To connect to your store emails, you may have to verify the email address you have added under "General settings" in your Shopify Admin. After that, you will receive your Shopify domain emails in your regular private email inbox.

[1.2.29]

Method 2. Email Address in a Third-Party Provider Connected to Shopify - G-Suite or Zoho

NOTE: It is easy to set up your Zoho or G-Suite accounts. But if you find it difficult, contact Google customer support for help. They will lead you through the process step by step.

Step 1. Connect existing domain

Click on your existing domain name in Shopify to open the details of the domain name.

[1.2.29a]

Scroll to the bottom of the dashboard and click on 'Third-party email hosting.'

[1.2.29b]

Either the Zoho or Gsuite websites will open and now you can add your business email.

Step 2. Connect to your hosting company

Follow the instructions to set up your email. You will get a 'metatag text' from a third-party email host, e.g., G-Suite, that you need to copy and paste into the text box in Shopify when prompted.

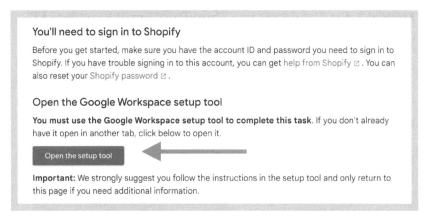

You'll need to sign in to Shopify

Before you get started, make sure you have the account ID and password you need to sign in to Shopify. If you have trouble signing in to this account, you can get help from Shopify ⬚ . You can also reset your Shopify password ⬚ .

Open the Google Workspace setup tool

You must use the Google Workspace setup tool to complete this task. If you don't already have it open in another tab, click below to open it.

Open the setup tool

Important: We strongly suggest you follow the instructions in the setup tool and only return to this page if you need additional information.

[1.2.36]

The relevant MX records will be added automatically.

MX RECORD			
Name	Points to	Priority	
@	mx.zoho.com	10	Actions
@	mx2.zoho.com	20	Actions
@	mx3.zoho.com	50	Actions

[1.2.35]

Step 3. Verify Email Address

If you have added your business email to your Shopify store, the email address must be verified.

Method 3. Email Address in a Third-Party Email Provider - I.E., GoDaddy

Step 1. Connect Existing Domain

Click on 'Connect Existing Domain' as shown below. Next, add your preferred domain name and verify.

[1.2.30]

Step 2. Connect To Your Hosting Company

If your domain is registered with a Shopify-partnered hosting company, your hosting company name will appear. See the following image to see what happens.

[1.2.31]

Your Shopify-partnered hosting company will automatically connect your domain name to Shopify and create all the appropriate DNS (domain name server) entries.

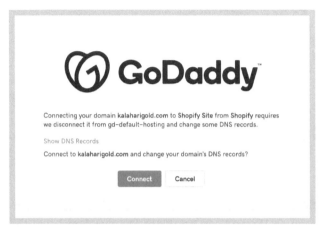

[1.2.32]

If you are not automatically connected to Shopify by your hosting provider when prompted, follow the instructions Shopify provides or get an expert to help – check on my website and ask.

Your hosting provider support should be proficient in adding the information to your domain.

Step 3. Verify Email Address

If you added a private email address when you registered your Shopify store you will need to verify a domain name (business) email address.

[1.3.6]

Now, the private email address you have added will not be shown to the customer. If you keep your private email address, then your customer will see that the email is sent via shopifyemail.com.

With all the spam online, I suggest adding a business email to your Shopify store. It will add to your brand recognition as well.

If you have added a private email and you want to add a business email address, click on the **domain section** to see who your host is if you do not know.

If you have not added a business or domain name email in Shopify, your customers will receive an email 'veronica.jeans@gmail.com via shopifyemail.com' in their inbox. The reason is to stop emails from disappearing into the SPAM folder.

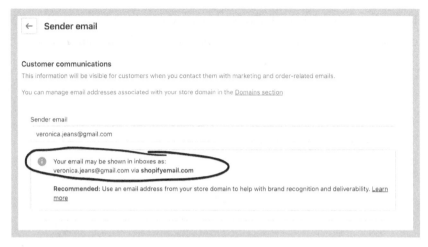

[1.2.37]

If you have a Shopify-hosted domain, then you don't need to do any additional setup to send from an email address associated with your store's domain.

Shopify will ask you to 'Fix it' if you have not verified your email address.

[1.2.34]

In the following image, I show a personal email address for Shopify customer service and a business email address for my customers.

[1.2.33]

The next image shows how you will verify your email address.

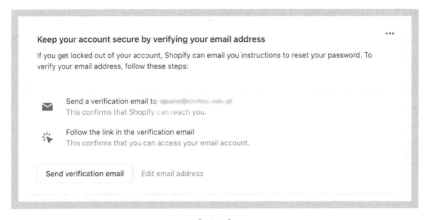

[1.2.41]

Step 4. Authenticate email address

In this window, you can see that your business email address is not authenticated yet.

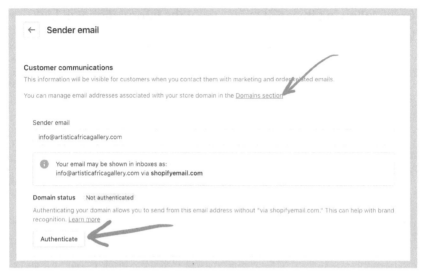

[1.2.38]

To authenticate your domain, you will need to create 4 new records with your domain provider:

1. *In a separate browser window, log in to the admin of your domain provider.*
2. *Navigate to the area of your domain provider settings for DNS management (this may be called a zone editor or cPanel).*
3. *In your domain provider's site, create 4 new CNAME records with the host names and values below. (You do not need to edit the TTL settings).*
4. *Provide each new CNAME record with both:*
5. *Host name: May also be called a "label" or "prefix"*
6. *Value: The URL destination your record points to*

In the following image, it shows what the information will look like.

[1.2.39]

If you click on the **domain settings** link, you will be able to see if your domain name is hosted with Shopify or a third-party host.

[1.2.40]

You might have to get your web developer or support from your third-party host to add information to your DNS settings.

Shopify will give you the exact DNS information that you need to add to your DNS settings with your third-party host.

Information on Shopify DNS for emails:

Record #1		
Type	CNAME	
Host name	u41._domainkey	Copy
Value	dkim1.cd5c528d833b.p578.email.myshopify.com	Copy

[1.2.39]

NOTE: Email alias and emails will work once you have started on a Shopify subscription.

RESOURCES:

Here is a link to my TOOLS page: **https://veronicajeans.online/ resources**

https://help.shopify.com/en/manual/domains/add-a-domain/ connecting-domains#add-an-existing-domain-to-your-shopify-store

Zoho Email Address information:

https://www.zoho.com/mail/help/adminconsole/shopify.html

Google Suite Email Address information:

https://workspace.google.com/intl/en_ca/products/gmail/

CHAPTER 3

SET UP YOUR BUSINESS INFORMATION IN SHOPIFY

WHERE *to find this in Shopify? Settings*

In this chapter you will verify your business information, choose a Shopify subscription plan and add your staff to your Shopify store.

The business information will affect your payments, shipping, and policies in your Shopify store. As you are entering the information, Shopify will automatically add it to the appropriate areas.

What to Expect in This Chapter:

- *Store Details*
- *Plans*
- *Users & Permissions*

STORE DETAILS

Where to find this in Shopify? Settings > Store Details

Once you have registered your Shopify store, proceed to '*Settings*' in your dashboard, which is at the bottom left of the Shopify dashboard.

[1.3.1]

Step 1. Verify or change store information

Once you are in your *'Settings'* dashboard, you will view the information you have added to your Shopify store when registering your Shopify store.

- *Profile (Basic information)*
- *Billing Information (Business Address)*
- *Store Currency*
- *Standards and formats*

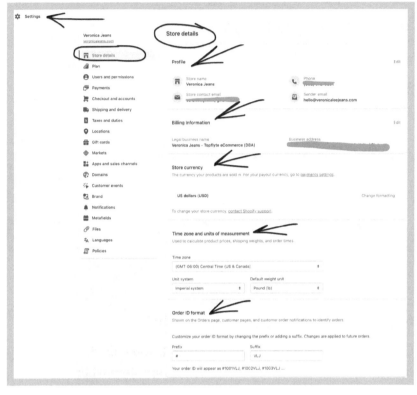

[1.3.2]

Step 2. Profile

Change the name of your store.

As per the following image, the store name was added, and this exact name will be added to all your brand as you logo wherever that is in Shopify.

You can always change the name of your store.

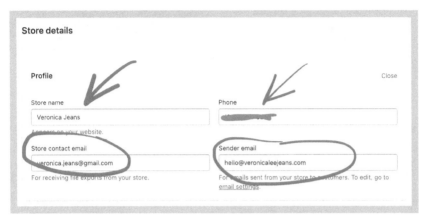

[1.3.9a]

My store name is 'Veronica Jeans' so that is what I added to my details.

Business phone number

The phone number you add here is the phone number for your customers to contact you. Remember, you will need to answer your phone as a business, and the voicemail will reflect your business name.

> Pro Tip: If you do not have a dedicated business phone number, you can get a free or cheap Google voice number that will also provide a voicemail.

Personal email address

If you added a private email address when registering your Shopify store, you must verify a domain name (business) email address.

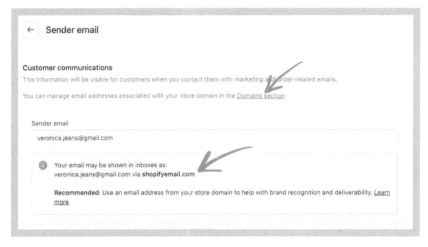

[1.3.7]

Business email address (Shopify)

If you register your domain with Shopify - Boom, done!

Sender email

hello@veronicaleejeans.com

Customers see this if you email them

[1.2.13

Step 3. Billing Information

When you registered your Shopify store, the details were automatically added to your basic details. If you want to change your information, go to '*Edit*' in the top right corner.

Essential information for your business will be reflected in your invoices to your customer, labels, and packaging invoice.

This address will also be allocated to your shipping location and affect how your customers will be taxed at checkout.

[1.3.9]

Add Your Legal Business Name

This is not your brand name but the legal business name that you registered for your business. Add the legal business name that you registered in your state or country.

Business address

Add your country and address. If you don't have a business address, you will have time to add this later.

> Pro Tip: You can add your P.O.Box number in this section, but it will be added to your default fulfillment location in your shipping setting. You can change this in 'Shipping and delivery.'

> Pro Tip: If you do not want to add your home address, a good suggestion is to get a UPS box and you can use the UPS store business address.

When you register a United States address, your store automatically has Shopify payments available.

If you add a different country than the United States, you will have different merchant payment and shipping options available.

NOTE: Your primary business location could affect which apps can be used in your store.

Shopify says: *"Not every app is built to work on every store. Some apps are designed to work with specific store settings. To prevent you from installing apps that don't work on your store, app developers can set installation requirements for their apps."*

Step 4. Store currency

Select the currency you want to use to sell your products in your store. After your first sale, the currency is locked in and can only be changed when you call Shopify support. To change your payout currency (the currency you want to receive into your bank account), go to the chapter about Payments.

Store currency
The currency your products are sold in. For your payout currency, go to payments settings

Store currency

Namibian dollars (NAD)   ⬍   Change formatting

[1.3.8]

If you want to change the formatting of how the currency will be displayed in your store. I suggest leaving this as is unless you have experience in coding.

[1.3.13]

Step 5. Time zone and units of measurement

Used to calculate product prices, shipping weights, and order times.

Add your unit system according to what your customers will be using.

- *If your primary customers are in the United States, Liberia or Myanmar, the format will be the old imperial system where things are measured in feet, inches, and pounds.*
- *If your primary customers are in other parts of the world, the format will be the new imperial system (metric).*

[1.3.11a]

Step 6. Order ID format

If you want to change the formatting of how the currency will be displayed in your store. I suggest leaving this as is unless you have experience in coding.

[1.3.11b]

PLANS

**Where to find this in Shopify? Settings > Plans*

The plan you choose for your Shopify store depends on your number of products, the credit card rate you want to pay, and other requirements your business needs.

Step 1. Choose your Shopify plan

Start with a basic plan unless you have a retail store and want to connect a POS (point of sale) system to your Shopify online store.

You will quickly realize which Shopify plan you need to get your information uploaded into your store.

> Pro Tip: Shopify support is very helpful if you need more clarity on the type of plan.

[1.3.14]

Let's get a quick look at the Shopify plans.

- *Basic Shopify Plan: Start selling your products online with your secure, beautiful store and in person at events, fairs, or markets.*
- *Shopify Plan: Add features like gift cards, retail hardware support, and professional reports to sell online or at a retail store.*
- *Advanced Shopify Plan: Scale your business online and in-person with advanced reporting and third-party calculated shipping rates.*

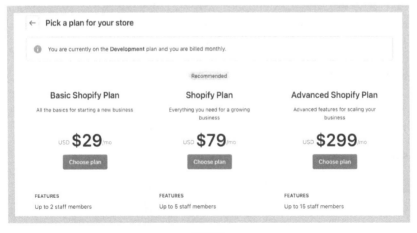

[1.3.15]

- *You can also create a Shopify Lite: You do not have an online store, pages, or landing pages. This function can be used as a 'Buy Button' in a blog or other page/site. To implement this payment option, you need to remove your 'Online Store.'*

[1.3.15a]

Shopify says: *"If you are on a trial plan and decide to sign up for a plan, or if you are looking to change the plan that you are on, then you can do so from the Settings page in your admin.*

If you update your plan, then a bill is issued immediately, reflecting only the subscription fee for your new plan. The price of your previous plan is prorated and applied against the cost of your new subscription for the month you change your plan. The bill you receive for your plan change does not include other pending charges on your account. These charges will be billed when outstanding fees on your account reach your billing threshold or at the end of your billing cycle."

Scroll down to the bottom of the Shopify plan detail page.

You can use your 'Buy Buttons' to sell on other websites or blogs. I will elaborate more in my Shopify Optimization series of books.

Step 2. Change next billing date

You can change your billing date. You can change your billing information only for monthly, yearly, 2 years, or 3 years.

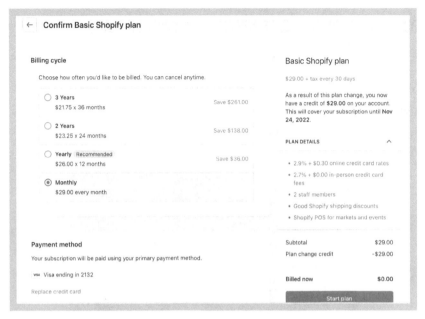

[1.3.17]

BONUS STEP: POINT OF SALE APP AND SUBSCRIPTION PLANS

**Where to find this in Shopify? Settings > Apps and sales channels

You might not be ready for to sell your products at events or in person, but because we are covering Shopify plans & subscriptions, I have added it to this book.

[1.3.28]

POS Lite: Accept casual, in-person payments at markets, fairs, pop-ups, and more.

POS Pro: Shopify POS Pro syncs with Shopify to track your orders and inventory across your retail locations, online store, and other active sales channels. This will entail Shopify hardware implementation.

[1.3.29]

Step 2. Change next billing date

You can change your billing date. You can change your billing information only for monthly, yearly, 2 years, or 3 years.

Billing and payout details and information is accessible on the main dashboard.

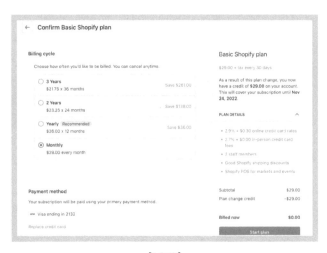

[1.3.17]

Step 3. Add details for your payment methods

This section will add your credit card details used to activate a Shopify plan.

If you activate any Apps, your payment or subscription will be added to the credit card on file, including your Shopify shipping, labels, and shipping charges.

[1.3.18]

USERS & PERMISSIONS

Where to find this in Shopify? Settings > Users & Permissions

[1.3.20]

What are the different users in Shopify?

Store owner: You are the store owner, and if you are not, and this is your business, make sure that gets changed. As the store owner, you have access to all the billing, finances, and banking information. You can also transfer ownership to another person.

Staff: Each plan has a different number of staff accounts you can create. Your team or staff can use these accounts to help you with your store. To add more accounts to your store, you need to give each person email access.

Collaborators: Collaborators are designers, developers, and marketers with access to your Shopify admin. They don't count toward your staff limit.

Step 1. Add a staff account

You can give your staff access to specific apps and sales channels, including different areas in your Shopify admin.

Add their name and email address to the prompt. Shopify will send them an email to verify access. The staff will create their password and have access to your Shopify store. Make sure you allocate the correct permissions to the different sections of your store.

[1.3.21]

Step 2. Set permissions for a staff account

Shopify says: "*Your Shopify pricing plan determines the number of staff members you can create:*

The Shopify Lite plan includes 1 staff member. The Basic Shopify plan includes 2 staff members. The Shopify plan includes 5 staff members.

The Advanced Shopify plan includes 15 staff members. The Shopify Plus plan includes unlimited staff members.

A staff member can have one of the following levels of permissions:

Owner permissions - Allows unlimited access to a Shopify store. The staff member can manage the account and the financial information for the store. There can only be one store owner at a time. By default, this is the person that initially opened the Shopify store.

Full permissions - Allows access to all sections of a Shopify store, apart from a sensitive account or financial information.

Limited permissions - Restricts a user to specified sections of your store. When you restrict a staff member from a section of the admin, they still see it in the sidebar of the admin, but they can't click or view any part of that section. For example, if you restrict a staff member from accessing your Settings page, then you also restrict them from accessing the shipping and tax settings.

The reasons for using limited permissions for staff will be different for each store. For example, you might want to use staff permissions in the following cases:

You don't want staff members to see any of your sales information, such as sales by month or sales by staff on the Reports page.

You don't want staff members to access any sensitive apps that might affect your business on the Apps page.

You don't want staff members to change any of your general store settings, such as your store address or your credit card information on the Settings page.

Store owners can give staff permission to log in to Shopify admin, but they can't edit their details."

The following images show the variety of permissions that can be set:

You need to add permissions for each staff or member. Select each permission or 'Select All' for admins. You control the permissions to your store.

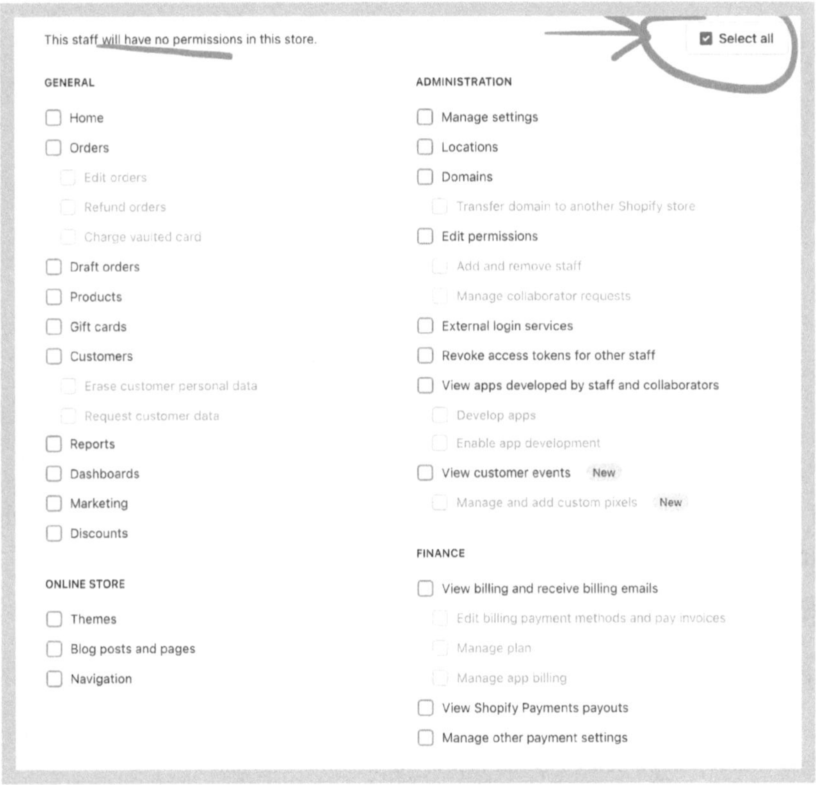

[1.3.22]

Permissions can be set for all Apps, App charges or individual Apps.

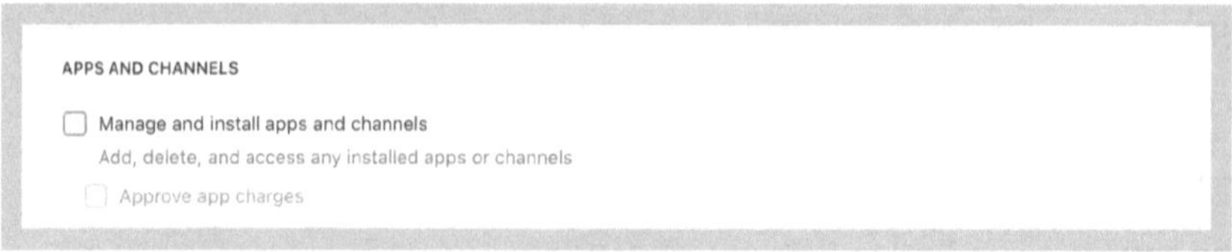

[1.3.24]

If you have a POS plan, then here is where you can set the POS staff permission. Either you allocate a pin or a random pin will be generated for each staff member.

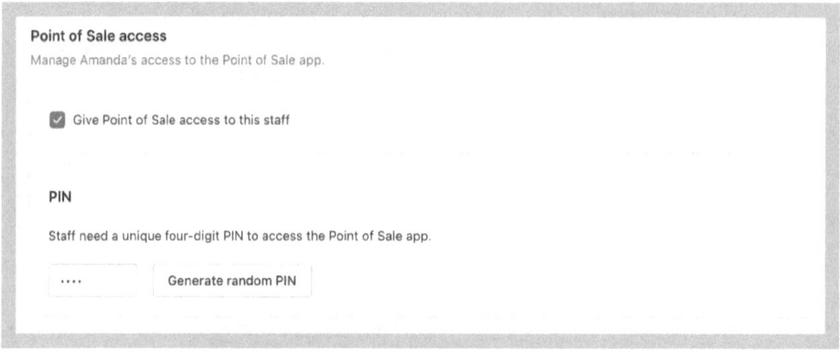

[1.3.25]

I have attached a link to view the Shopify staff permissions in detail in the Resources section at the end of the chapter.

Step 3. Add collaborators

There are two ways to allow these to work in your Shopify store:

- *Anyone can send a collaborator request.*
- *Only people with a collaborator request code can send a collaborator request.*

Collaborators

These give designers, developers, and marketers access to your Shopify admin. They don't count toward your staff limit. Learn more about collaborators.

○ Anyone can send a collaborator request
◉ Only people with a collaborator request code can send a collaborator request

COLLABORATOR REQUEST CODE   Generate new code

3655

Share this code to allow someone to send you a collaborator request. You'll still need to review and approve their request.

[1.3.26]

> Pro Tip: Always verify who is allowed in your account and restrict permissions. Nobody needs access to your customers, orders or finances.

Step 4. Login services

You can allow staff to use Google apps to log into Shopify. It is not necessary to allocate this to your admin or staff.

Login services
Allow staff to use external services to log in to Shopify.

Name	Status	
Google Apps	Disabled: Staff can't use Google Apps to log in	Edit

[1.3.27]

RESOURCES:

Here is a link to my TOOLS page: **https://veronicajeans.online/resources**

View the Shopify staff permissions in detail. https://help.shopify.com/en/manual/your-account/staff-accounts/staff-permissions/staff-permissions-descriptions

TaxJar Sales Tax Guide:

https://developers.taxjar.com/integrations/guides/

Avalara Sales Tax Lookup: https://www.avalara.com/taxrates/en/state-rates.html

Learn more on Shopify - **https://veronicajeans.online/shopify-taxes**

You can check out Tax Jar or Avalara - the blogs are very informative but always verify your information before implementing any tax changes.

CHAPTER 4
PAYMENTS

**WHERE *to find this in Shopify? Setting > Payments*

One of the most important functions in your store is your financial information.

This chapter covers how you get paid, how much your merchant interest (%) rate is, and what payment options are available to your customers while they are shopping.

I have also included an explanation of the financial process from end to end. It is crucial to understand how your money moves and works to be successful in any endeavor.

What to Expect in This Chapter:

- *Information You Need Before You Start*
- *Payment Providers in Shopify*
- *Shopify Payments*
- *Additional Payment Methods*
- *Manual Payment Methods*
- *Your Shopify Store Payouts (Money)*
- *The Financial Process from End-to-End*

INFORMATION YOU NEED BEFORE YOU START

Collect this information before you start:

Bank Account information - router and bank account details at the bottom of a paper check or by contacting your bank.

Personal details associated with your Bank Account: Business owner, or a significant shareholder name, DOB (Date of Birth) and last 4 digits of the Social Security number (This information is required to verify your identity).

Legal Company Name - your registered company name with State or Local authority and company address. If you have a home business, you would add the business address you registered with your State or Local authority.

Company EIN - An Employer Identification Number (EIN) is a unique identification number assigned to a business entity so that it can easily be identified by the Internal Revenue Service (IRS). It is your tax identification number when you file your yearly taxes. The EIN is also known as a Federal Tax Identification Number. If you are a DBA (Doing Business As), you DO NOT need an EIN. Your Social Security number is sufficient. Please get advice from an accountant if you are doing business as a sole proprietor or individual. This can have significant tax implications for your personal income tax.

PAYMENT PROVIDERS IN SHOPIFY

Getting paid by your customers requires an understanding of the payment process. When a customer checks out, they can choose from any of the payment methods you've enabled in the Payment Provider area of your Shopify admin. Shopify supports a variety of payment methods.

When choosing payment methods, you should consider a few factors. If you want to let customers pay with a credit card, you can use **Shopify Payments or a third-party service.**

PayPal, Amazon Pay, Google Pay, and Apple Pay (and more) are also ways for customers to pay online without using a credit card. Cryptocurrency is another option you might want to consider.

Your business location and where your customers live should be taken into account when choosing a payment provider. Find out which payment gateways are available in your country and what currencies they support by browsing Shopify's list of payment gateways by country.

SHOPIFY PAYMENTS

**Where to find this in Shopify? Setting > Payments > Shopify Payments

The following payment providers are available in Shopify:

- *PayPal Express*
- *Amazon Pay*
- *Third-Party Providers*
- *Cryptocurrencies and NFTs*
- *Manual Payment Methods*

Shopify is available to you in most countries.

NOTE: *A security option in Shopify is that only the store owner can view payment information about the business.*

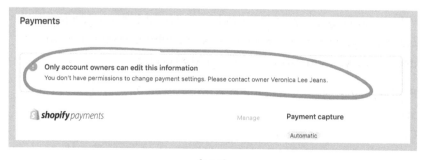

[1.4.1]

If you are doing business in the USA and your business address is in the USA, then 'Shopify Payments' is available for your store. If you have registered your Shopify store outside of the USA, you will not be able to use Shopify Payments.

Shopify Payment is easy to set up because this payment option is a merchant account and a gateway in one system.

Before accepting payments on your store, you'll need to provide some information on your business and its ownership. Shopify might require some additional information if your business cannot be verified. So be sure to add the correct business information.

SHOPIFY PAYMENTS

Step 1. Activate Shopify payments

First, click on the button 'Activate Shopify Payments.'

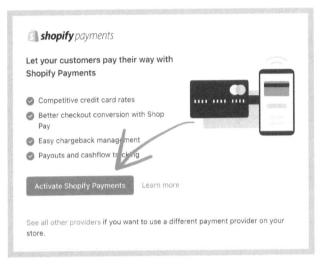

[1.4.2]

Step 2. Add business details

Choose the type of business you are registered for in your state or country in the dropdown. And there are different requirements for each type of business.

If you are a sole proprietor/individual, you will only need your Social Security Number for your registration. This information is the same as when you created a business bank account with your bank.

If you are a single-member LLC, you will need Employer Identification Number (EIN) or Social Security number (SSN).

If you are a corporation, partnership, or non-profit, you will need your EIN (Employer Identification Number) for these entries. This information will also reflect on your business bank account.

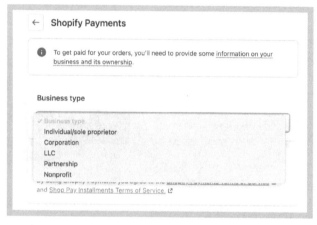

[1.4.3a]

If you are not a sole proprietor, your business needs to be verified

To comply with financial regulations in your country, you need to provide more information about your business and the individuals associated with your business.

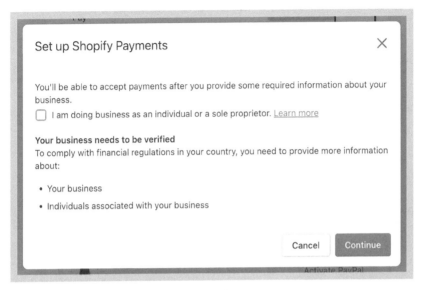

[1.4.3b]

The information for your business will be in step 3.

If you are an individual, the EIN is optional.

Fill in your business address reflected on your bank statement and business registration papers.

Business type

Individual/sole proprietor   ⬍

Business details

Employer Identification Number (EIN) (optional)

9 digits

Street address

1900 SHIPYARD DR, 5

City   ZIP code

Seabrook   77586-3469

State

Texas   ⬍

[1.4.3]

> Pro Tip: Do not use a personal bank
> account for business. Separate your
> personal and business banking right from
> the start. Consult your CPA or your banker.

Step 3. Add personal details

Fill out the personal information of the person associated with the
business bank account, a business owner, or significant
shareholder.

Personal details

The person associated with your account should be a business owner or significant shareholder.

First name

Veronica Jeans,

Last name

Shopify Queen & Bestselling Author

Date of birth

Month   Day   Year

Last 4 digits of your Social Security number (SSN)

This information is required to verify your identity.

[1.4.4]

Pro Tip: Add the correct information, it can be difficult to prove you are the owner of this business/store to Shopify.

Step 4. Additional owners

If you are the sole owner of your business, check the correct option and there is not need to add any other information.

Additional owners

Please enter the details of any individual who owns 25% or more of the company

⦿ I am the only owner

◯ Add another owner, or a director

[1.4.5]

If you have a Partner LLC or an Incorporation, add your additional owners to the information.

Personal Information - Name & Email address.

And the % of ownership in the business.

[1.4.5a]

NOTE: This is all public information, so you are to disclose private information. Shopify is trying to prevent people from opening a store and spamming consumers.

Step 5. Add product details

Enter the type of products you are going to sell. For the business category, the obvious choice will be 'Retail' if you are selling products. Then select the subcategory, which indicates what niche market you are serving.

For instance: fashion, shoes, kid's clothes, boutiques, skincare, industrial fittings, etc.

Product details

Business category

Retail

Business subcategory

Books

Description of products or services

[1.4.6]

Step 6. Add the customer billing statement details

This section is for your customer's billing statement. The information that you add here will appear on their bank statement. Edit your store name and phone number.

Customer billing statement

Edit the way your store name and phone number appear on your customers' bank statements.

Statement descriptor

SP * KALAHARIGOLD

Phone number

+1 |

[1.4.7]

Step 7. Add your banking information

Add the bank account where you want Shopify to deposit your money. Double-check the numbers you add to this box because you don't want somebody else to receive your payments.

Banking information

Your funds will be deposited into this bank account.

Routing number

Account number

Routing   Account

✔ 088 ✔ ⑆ 123456789 ⑆   123456789 ✔

These numbers can be found at the bottom of a check or by contacting your bank.

[1.4.8]

Step 8. Complete your account setup

Read through the terms of service. Always know what terms and conditions you agree to. Shopify payment terms are a standard agreement with any merchant or banking company.

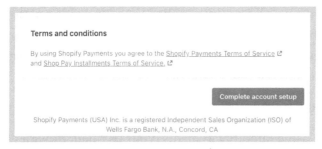

Terms and conditions

By using Shopify Payments you agree to the Shopify Payments Terms of Service ↗ and Shop Pay Installments Terms of Service. ↗

Complete account setup

Shopify Payments (USA) Inc. is a registered Independent Sales Organization (ISO) of Wells Fargo Bank, N.A., Concord, CA

[1.4.9]

Pro Tip: Make sure information is correct the first time. It is not easy to change some information after the fact. For example, your business details, personal details, and product descriptions are unavailable for change.

Step 9. Manage Shopify Payments

Once you have set up your Shopify Payments, there is another step. Navigate back to the main Payment window.

Click on 'Manage' in the Shopify Payment section.

shopify payments

Manage

VISA   AMEX   DISC●VER   (I)   ❐Pay   ✦Pay   G Pay   ∞Meta

Credit card rate   Transaction fee
As low as 2.9% + $0.30   0%

ℹ You can get improved Shopify Payments rates by upgrading your Shopify plan.

PAYOUT BANK ACCOUNT

Your payouts are scheduled for every business day and are deposited into bank account ****** 96 (USD)

View payouts

[1.4.10]

Once you have all your information in the system, you can see your rates, what credit card choices you offer your customers, and your payout banking information. Next, we need to add or change some things in your Shopify Payments.

Standard Rates

If you're using Shopify Payments (your payment provider is 'Shopify Payments,' which is not to be confused with Shopify), transaction fees don't apply to orders.

Transaction fees also don't apply to manual payment methods. Manual payment methods include cash on delivery (COD), bank deposits, checks, test orders, and draft orders marked as paid or pending. Transaction fees don't apply to POS orders.

If you don't use Shopify Payments or the manual payment method, then transaction fees apply for orders in addition to the processing fee charged by your payment provider.

Your account is billed depending on your store's transaction volume, Recurring App charges, and the payment provider you use.

In the following image you will see the rates (%) and an authorization fee (.30), but no transaction fee.

Standard rates

The rates are dependent on your Shopify plan and apply to all payment methods unless otherwise shown.

	Online	In-person
Domestic	2.9% + $0.30	2.7% + $0.00
Rest of world	3.9% + $0.30	2.7% + $0.00

[1.4.11]

Step 10. Accepted payment options

In this step, all accepted payment options are included.

Accepted Payment options with Shopify Payments are seen in the following image. You can choose which ones you want to use. Give your customers every opportunity to pay you.

[1.4.12]

Step 11. Accelerated checkout with payment options

Shop Pay is another option offered by Shopify and makes it easier for customers to pay for their products quickly. Test it and see how it works once you are Live.

Shop Pay Installments allows your customers to buy everything in their cart and pay with free installments. The cool part is that you get your money, and Shop Pay collects the money from the customer.

The Shop Pay option is a great asset to add to your store to improve conversions.

[1.4.13]

Once set up, you can add Shop Pay Installments, a Sales App in Shopify.

[1.4.14]

Step 12. Digital wallets

Wallets are a digital way for customers to pay you via their mobile. Your visitor does not have to get a credit card; it is already programmed into their phone.

Wallets

Shopify Payments accepts digital wallet payments to help you increase conversion on mobile.

☑	⬛ Pay	Apple Pay		Card rates apply
☑	⬛ Pay	Google Pay		Card rates apply
☑	⬛ Meta	Meta Pay		Card rates apply

[1.4.15]

Step 13. International - currencies & pricing

You can accept payment in different currencies. Your amounts are automatically converted based on the foreign exchange rate and the Shopify rounding rules.

Add different currencies to your online store so international visitors can shop and pay in their local currency.

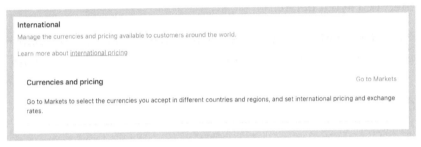

International
Manage the currencies and pricing available to customers around the world.

Learn more about international pricing

Currencies and pricing   Go to Markets

Go to Markets to select the currencies you accept in different countries and regions, and set international pricing and exchange rates.

[1.4.16]

Shopify says: *"Selling in multiple currencies lets your customers pay for their orders using their currency. This feature is a good option when your business is in one of the following situations:*

You have one online store with international traffic, and you want to increase your conversions from your international customers.

You want to offer regional stores. For example, you have a store in one region, and you'd like to sell to customers who live in a similar region but use a different currency. For example, Australia and New Zealand are similar in that they are geographically close and share the same seasons. You could use selling in multiple currencies to sell in Australia and offer a regional experience for your New Zealand customers.

You have a strong international presence with stores in different countries and regions. You have one international store that uses selling in multiple currencies to convert customers where you don't have a specific presence yet."

> Pro Tip: Start with one market first before
> you start expanding your business. Get to
> know all the intricacies of running an online
> store before adding more capabilities to
> your store.

NOTE: *This is managed in the 'Market' section and the set up is available in Shopify - Optimize your Shopify Store book.*

Step 14. Payout details

Payout account: The bank account allocated in Shopify is the bank account where you want to receive payments from the sale of your products in your store. Here is where you can change your bank account details.

Payout details
Your earnings are deposited into this bank account. Choose the frequency of your payouts and edit the way they're described on your bank statements.

Payout bank account

🏛 ****** 96 (USD)

Change bank account

[1.4.17]

Payout statement descriptor:

This descriptor is a great way to identify the payments from your store in your bank account statement. If you have several stores, you can distinguish between store payments.

Payout statement descriptor

The way payouts are described on your bank statements.

Payout statement descriptor

Shopify

Must be between 5 and 22 characters

[1.4.18]

Payout schedule: Depending on your preferences, you can schedule payouts from Shopify to your bank account daily, every week on a specific day, or once a month.

Don't forget to check the email notifications. You get notified when money has been deposited into your bank account.

Payout schedule

◉ Every business day
○ Every week

on Monday

○ Every month

on day 1

☑ Enable notifications
Get notified by email every time you receive a payout

[1.4.19]

Step 15. Fraud prevention

Reduce your store's risk of credit card fraud by adding extra security.

Automatically decline charges

Shopify Payments has excellent fraud protection in place for your store. I usually check both options. But you can choose either or none.

Why would you decline when the AVS postal code verification fails? This will inform you that your customer has different shipping addresses. I always check via the address in 'Orders.' It adds a small layer of security for the credit card user and your store. It allows you to connect with your customer and ensure their products go to the preferred address.

The second option is a standard fraud protection verification. I would definitely leave that one in place.

Fraud prevention
Reduce your store's risk of credit card fraud by adding extra security.

Automatically decline charges   Learn more

☑ Decline charges that fail AVS postal code verification

☑ Decline charges that fail CVV verification

[1.4.20]

I suggest enabling both these boxes, which is the inherent fraud protection in Shopify.

Shopify says: "*Address Verification System (AVS) - AVS compares the numeric part of the customer's billing address and zip code or postal code to the information on file with the credit card issuer. This helps reduce a significant amount of fraud because unauthorized users often don't have the correct billing address.*

Card Verification Value (CVV) - The CVV is a 3-digit or 4-digit number on the back of the customer's credit card. Credit card companies prohibit the storage of the CVV code, so asking for the CVV is a way of ensuring that a customer has the card physically in their possession. Credit card information stolen from a merchant database is also less useful because it shouldn't contain CVV information."

What happens when a payment is not verified?

A payment error notification is sent automatically to the customer if their payment can't be processed during checkout.

Pending payment error: Sent automatically to the customer if their pending payment can't be processed after checking out.

Pending payment success: Sent automatically to the customer when their pending payment is successfully processed after checking out.

Step 16. Customer billing statement

Shopify will automatically add your company information, but you can change this to whatever you want. It is a good idea to have your company name in the statement because they can see what store they bought from but also, your name pops up for them again, which is part of marketing.

[1.4.21]

Step 17. Test Mode

Before you start your store, create a payment in Test Mode. The charge will not get processed, but you can see and practice how to process your orders and ensure your checkout works the way you want. The following image shows how to simulate your payments and online orders.

Test mode

Test Shopify Payments setup and configuration to simulate successful and failed transactions. Learn more about test mode ⤴ .

Test mode

☐ Enable test mode

Deactivate Shopify Payments   Switch to a third-party provider   **Save**

[1.4.22]

Step 18. Simulate successful transactions

Simulating some transactions allows you to test your system and get used to the order processing before you go live with your store.

From the Shopify support page: "*To simulate a successful transaction, use the following information when you are asked for credit card details at checkout:*"

Simulate successful transactions

To simulate a successful transaction, use the following information when you are asked for credit card details at checkout:

- **Name on card**: Enter at least two words.
- **Expiry date**: Enter any date in the future.
- **CVV**: Enter any three digits.
- **Card number**: Use any of the following numbers:

Card type	Test credit number
Visa	4242424242424242
Mastercard	5555555555554444
American Express	378282246310005
Discover	6011111111111117
Diners Club	30569309025904
JCB	3530111333300000

[1.4.23]

Step 19. Simulate failed transactions

Testing a failed transaction is as important as a successful transaction.

Shopify says: "*If you want to see the credit card error messages that might be displayed to a customer during checkout, then you can use these test credit card numbers to simulate different failed transactions:*

Use credit card number 4000000000000002 to generate a card declined message.

Use credit card number 4242424242424241 to generate an incorrect number message.

Use credit card number 4000000000000259 to simulate a disputed transaction.

Use an invalid expiry month, for example, 13, to generate an invalid expiry month message.

Use an expiry year in the past to generate an invalid expiry year message.

Use a two-digit security code number to generate an invalid security code message."

NOTE: *When you go 'Live', remember to disable the Test Mode.*

Step 20. Verify your business with Shopify

You might get a verification email from Shopify to add more information to verify that you reside in the USA.

I reside and have my business in the USA, but my customers are in Namibia.

Here is the email that I received from Shopify:

To keep your Shopify Payments account up to date, you need to verify your identity by Tuesday, December 20, 2022 at 2:13 pm -0600.

If you don't verify your identity, you may lose the ability to accept payments on your store and you won't receive your payouts.

Verify identity

ℹ Learn how to verify your identity.

[1.4.27]

And here are the verification documents Shopify requires to be uploaded.

← Business verification

You need to submit additional details about your business to continue accepting payments.
Any information you submit is stored securely and only used for verification purposes. Learn more

Identity verification for Veronica Jeans Shopify Queen & Bestselling Author

Upload a copy of a valid government-issued photo ID by December 20, 2022 at 2:13 pm.

The document you submitted couldn't be verified. Please contact support to complete the verification.

Identity verification for Veronica Jeans Shopify Queen & Bestselling Author

Driver's License

Document front

Add file

Must be a .png, .jpg and be smaller than 8 MB

[1.4.28]

Not as difficult as it seems when you get the official email. Very easy to solve.

DOING BUSINESS IN EUROPE

Step 1. Add your own provider

If you are doing business in Europe and your business address is in Europe, you can add your payment provider with Shopify.

[1.4.40a]

Shopify suggests choosing Stripe. Or you can choose your own provider through the link at the bottom of the page as indicated in the following image.

[1.4.40b]

Shopify partners with Stripe for secure payments to make it easy for European businesses to set up a payment provider.

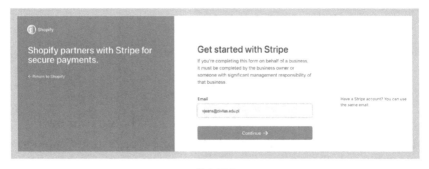

[1.4.40c]

Step 2. Verify your business with Shopify

You might get a verification email from Shopify to add more information to verify that you reside in the USA.

ADDITIONAL PAYMENT METHODS

**Where to find this in Shopify? Setting > Payments*

These are the additional payment methods in Shopify:

- *PayPal Express*
- *Amazon Pay*
- *Payment Methods & Providers (Third-Party Payment Providers)*
- *Cryptocurrencies*
- *NFT*

Shopify supports two types of credit card payment providers: direct and external. If you're using a direct provider, your customers can complete their purchases directly on your online store without having to pay at a third-party checkout. If you're using an external provider, your customers must complete their purchases on a checkout page hosted outside your online store.

Providers enable you to accept payment methods at a rate set by a third party. A 2% fee applies to payments processed through third-party providers, depending on your Shopify plan.

There are different reasons to use a third-party payment provider.

- *Suppose you sell CBD, cigarettes, drugs, guns, knives, and more. If you want to know if your product is on the list of products not allowed to use Shopify Payments, check out this Shopify page: https://help.shopify.com/en/manual/markets/markets-pro/prohibited-items*
- *IP Infringement, regulated or illegal products, and services. Shopify Payments is not restrictive; the law or the financial partners dictate what can or cannot be sold with particular merchant services.*
- *If you are an international company/business, you might have to use a third-party payment provider if Shopify Payments is not affiliated directly with a bank in your country.*
- *If you want to use different types of Cryptocurrencies.*
- *Crypto.com accepts over 20 cryptocurrencies, including Bitcoin, Ethereum, and Dogecoin.*

- Coinbase Commerce accepts a variety of cryptocurrencies including Bitcoin, Ethereum, Dogecoin, and more. Coinbase also allows for easy conversion to fiat.
- BitPay accepts 14 cryptocurrencies including Bitcoin, Bitcoin Lightning, Ethereum, and Dogecoin settled in USD.
- DePay accepts Ethereum, Binance Smart Chain, or Polygon tokens that have liquidity on decentralized exchanges. DePay is a peer-to-peer payment gateway that uses smart contracts for on-the-fly conversion.
- OpenNode accepts Bitcoin and Bitcoin Lightning settled in Bitcoin or fiat.
- Strike accepts Bitcoin Lightning settled in USD.
- If you want to use NFT - non-fungible tokens in your store. A non-fungible token (NFT) is a unique digital identifier recorded on the blockchain used to demonstrate proof of ownership of digital or physical goods.

Why do you get charged more?

- Shopify provides a safe and secure platform to process your payments. Your third-party provider will also charge fees to process your transactions.
- Shopify is not responsible for fraud or fees if you use a third-party provider.
- This option is for international stores or prohibitive products, e.g., Tobacco, CBD, etc. There is a list on the Shopify website.
- Providers enable you to accept payment methods at a rate set by a third party. A 2% fee applies to payments processed through third-party providers.

I will not show all the third-party payment providers because it is a long list. Investigate each one to see if they suit your business.

Pro Tip: If you don't see a third-party option for your business, many will create a connection to Shopify. This option might incur a considerable setup fee.

PAYPAL EXPRESS

A PayPal button in your store gives your customers more choices when shopping in your store. You want to make it as easy as possible for your customers to buy your products in whatever form they choose.

PayPal is one of Shopify's default payment providers. As soon as you open a store, you're given a PayPal Express Checkout account with the email you used to sign up for your Shopify store. Before you can collect payments for orders made with PayPal, you need to set up your PayPal account.

The only drawback with PayPal is that your money will not be automatically transferred to your bank account. Instead, you need to activate your payment transfers in PayPal manually.

This is the most straightforward payment to set up.

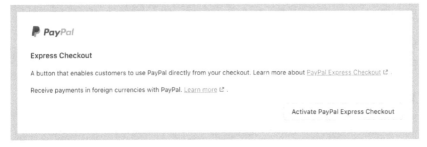

[1.4.25]

Step 1. Create a PayPal account

If you don't have a PayPal account, create one. If you have one, skip this step and go to the next step.

Go to PayPal.com and create your account. Just follow the prompts; it is easy to set up.

Create a personal or business account. You get more benefits and capabilities for your business from a business account and the cost does not change.

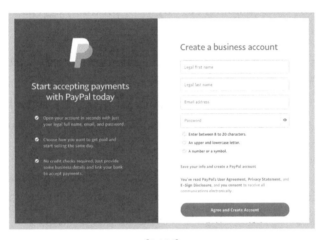

[1.4.26]

Step 2. Activate your PayPal account in Shopify

Hit 'Activate' and add the email address associated with your PayPal account.

You are connected.

AMAZON PAY

NOTE: Amazon Pay is only for stores in the United States.

Amazon Pay provides your customers with another secure way to pay you. Your customer will be logged into their Amazon account to pay with their credit card on file in Amazon.

This is not an Amazon Seller account. However, my Shopify Optimization series of books will discuss linking to your Amazon accounts.

You activate your Amazon Pay. I will not explain every step, but the images show you how and what you need to add this payment option to your Shopify store.

Just follow the prompts and add your information. You will need the same information that you needed to add to Shopify Payments so keep them handy.

Step 1. Activate Amazon Pay

In Shopify, click on the 'Activate Amazon Pay.'

[1.4.29]

Step 2. Register on the Amazon Pay website

Once you are on the website, register your account for Amazon Pay.

[1.4.30]

The Amazon Pay account will be added to your Amazon business accounts if you have an Amazon Seller account. If you do not, Amazon will create an overall account for you where you can add additional services.

[1.4.31]

Step 3. Add your business information

You can use the business information I advised you to collect for your Shopify Payments in this step.

In the following images, I have shown you how I registered my account with my information

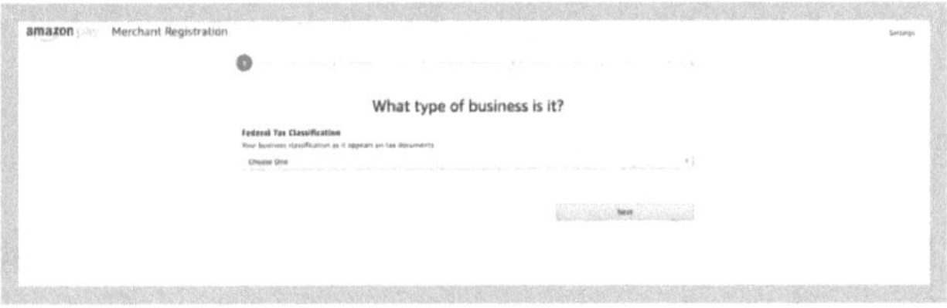

[1.4.32]

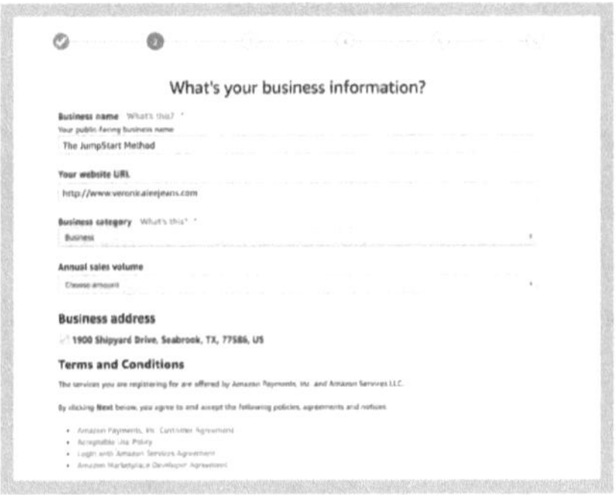

[1.4.33]

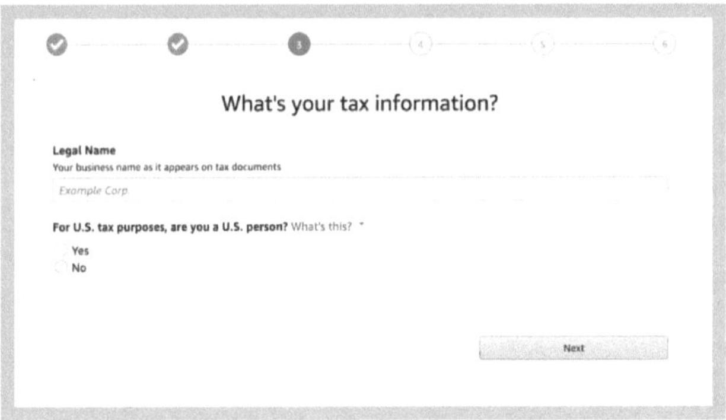

[1.4.34]

Step 4. Add a credit card

You need to add your credit card for authentication and also if you have any fees. Remember, this is part of the overall Amazon services and some of them have fees.

Amazon Pay does not require you to pay any fees. This is strictly as a convenience and trust factor for your customer.

What credit card do we keep on file?

(i) Why do we need your credit card?
Setting up your account costs nothing. Before you can receive disbursements, we require you to provide a credit card that Amazon Pay can charge if your account falls into a negative balance. *

Name on credit card

Credit card number   **Expiration date**
                                          MM / YY

Billing Address
☑ Use business address: 1900 Shipyard Drive, Seabrook, TX, 77586, US

Next

[1.4.35]

Step 5. Add your website address

You can add as many websites as you want to. These are the sites that you might use for Amazon pay services.

[1.4.36]

Step 6. Share your credentials with Shopify

Transfer credentials to your Shopify store. Your Amazon Pay merchant information will be shared with Shopify, which is the API and privacy keys that connect the 2 systems. It is automatic so you don't have to do anything.

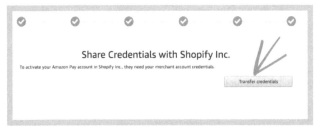

[1.4.37]

Once you have clicked the button, you are back in Shopify.

[1.4.38]

Step 7. Verification emails

This is what you will see in your email! Now your Amazon Pay is confirmed.

[1.4.39]

PAYMENT METHODS & PROVIDERS (THIRD-PARTY PAYMENT PROVIDERS)

**Where to find this in Shopify? Setting > Payments*

There are three methods for using third-party payment providers:

METHOD 1. BUSINESSES IN THE USA WITH PROHIBITED PRODUCTS

If you are registered in the USA and selling prohibited products, you need to choose a provider either in Shopify as the supported provider or a payment provider through a Shopify App.

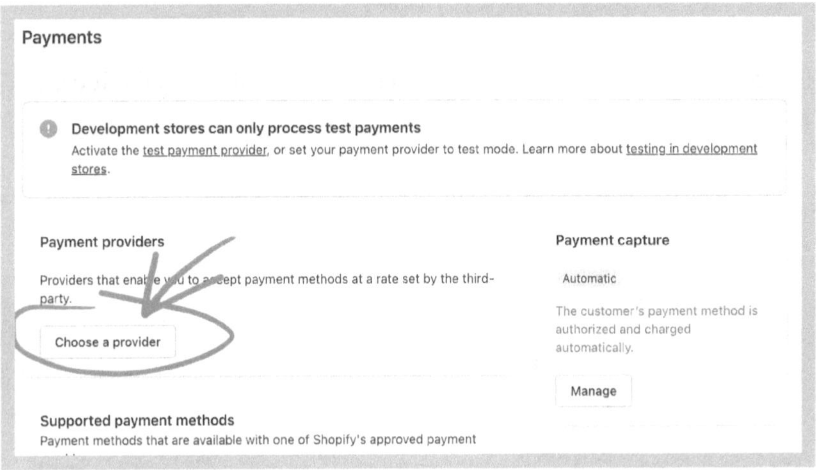

[1.4.40a]

Shopify suggests choosing Stripe or you can choose your own provider through the link at the bottom of the page as indicated in the following image.

[1.4.40b]

Shopify partners with Stripe for secure payments to make it easy for European businesses to set up a payment provider.

[1/4/40c]

Method 2. Business in the USA & a third-party payment provider

Where to find this in Shopify? Settings > Payments > Shopify Payments > Manage

If you are a registered USA business and you want to change from Shopify Payments to a third-party payment provider, you can navigate through your Shopify Payment portal. You might do this if you had QuickBooks payments already set up.

Navigate to the link at the bottom of the page.

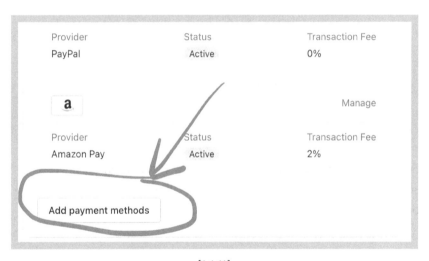

[1.4.40]

Click on 'Switch to a third-party provider' to get to the payment providers section.

Provider	Status	Transaction Fee
PayPal	Active	0%

a   Manage

Provider	Status	Transaction Fee
Amazon Pay	Active	2%

Add payment methods

[1.4.41]

METHOD 3. INTERNATIONAL BUSINESS NOT IN EUROPE & THIRD-PARTY PROVIDER

Where to find this in Shopify? Settings > Payments > Supported Payment Methods

Click on 'Add Payment Methods.'

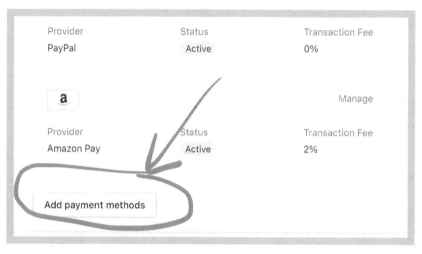

[1.4.41]

Search by Payment methods or search by a provider. When you search by provider, many payment providers will pop up. Choose one that fits your store.

[1.4.42]

Step 1. Add Payment Methods

Search for a payment provider or add a payment provider name to see if they are available. If your payment provider is not on the list, they might have an app that will link you to Shopify. For instance, Quicken merchant services are integrated with an app.

Step 2. Activate Your Payment Provider

Follow the prompts to activate your payment provider.

NOTE: These steps are beyond this Shopify book, but most providers require all the information you gathered and there might be an approval and verification stage.

CRYPTOCURRENCIES & NFTS

Cryptocurrencies and NFTs are recent additions to Shopify and eCommerce in general. They are not usual payments in an online store. As they are not universally available, it might restrict your customers from purchases.

NOTE: The next steps only show you how to find your currency, and you must follow the steps to add it to your store. Most providers require all the information you gathered, and there might be an approval and verification stage.

Cryptocurrencies

Cryptocurrencies are a form of digital or virtual currency that can be transferred directly from person to person over the internet.

Step 1. Add payment methods

If you want to add cryptocurrencies to your Shopify store, you will find them in the 'Additional payments' and click on the 'Add payment methods.'

[1.4.40b]

Step 2. Find your currency or provider

Find your currency and add to your Shopify store.

[1.4.40]

NFT - Non-fungible Token

A non-fungible token (NFT) is a unique digital identifier recorded on the blockchain used to demonstrate proof of ownership of digital or physical goods. NFTs can store publicly verifiable data related to ownership, transaction history, and provenance.

Blockchains are distributed databases or ledger systems managed by multiple computers, or nodes, on a network. Transactions are stored in data blocks, which are confirmed by the entire network. These data blocks are chained together to form a shared, trusted, and irreversible timeline of events.

NOTE: In this book I only want to explain what NFTs are but this is a big topic and beyond this set up for Shopify. Here is a resource for more information about NFTs: https://veronicajeans.online/NFT

MANUAL PAYMENT METHODS

Where to find this in Shopify? Setting > Payments

You can accept manual payments outside your online checkouts, such as money orders or bank transfers.

Some customers don't want to pay for their orders using a credit card. These customers can still place online orders if you set up a manual payment method. When your customers use a manual payment method, you can arrange to receive their payment outside your online checkout. After you receive the payment, you can then manually approve the order. Common types of manual payments include cash on delivery (COD), money orders, and bank transfers. You can accept email money transfers if your store and your customers are based in Canada.

Unless you activate Shopify Payments as your payment provider, you'll be charged transaction fees for all orders that aren't brokered financially by Shopify. This includes orders that go through Shopify's checkout system with your third-party provider.

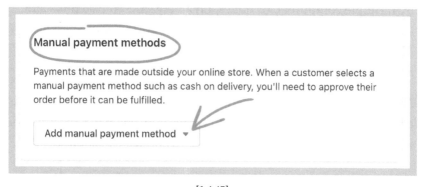

[1.4.45]

Here are the different 'Manual Payments' you can activate:

- *Create a Custom Payment Method*

- *Cash On Delivery (COD)*
- *Bank Deposit*
- *Money Order*

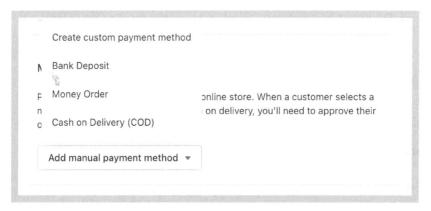

[1.4.46]

Step 1. Choose a manual payment method

If you choose 'Custom Payment Method' you can give a custom name to the payment method.

[1.4.47]

Add the next information:

- *Additional details* - *displays to customers when choosing a payment method on the checkout.*
- *Payment instructions* - *displays to customers after they place an order.*

As with the other manual payment methods – cash on delivery, bank deposit, and money order, you will need to add additional details and payment instructions for your customers to pay you.

Step 2. Activate payment method

Done!

CAPTURE PAYMENTS

**Where to find this in Shopify? Setting > Payments

Shopify says: "*When a customer makes a payment using a credit card, the payment information needs to be captured and sent to their bank for processing. If you are using Shopify Payments or another credit card payment provider, then you'll need to decide how to capture payment from your customers.*"

Step 1. Manage capture payment

Click on 'Manage' and you can now choose or change how you want to capture payments made during a sale.

[1.4.24]

Choose between:

Method 1. Automatically capture payment for orders.

The customer's payment method is authorized and charged automatically. The system immediately captures payments made at the time of the sale. This is automatic choice by Shopify, so you do not have to do anything.

Method 2. Manually capture payment for orders.

The customer's payment method is authorized at the time of their order. You'll need to capture payment within the authorized period manually.

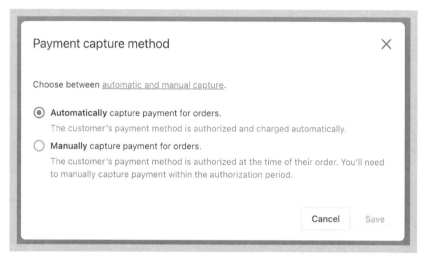

[1.4.24a]

Two examples of why you might choose to capture payments manually:

- *If you create your own handmade products, and you only want to take payment when the product is completed and ready to ship.*
- *If you are drop-shipping your products, and you only want to charge the customer when your drop shipping has been approved.*

The extra step would be to capture the payments within the authorized period.

Shopify says: *"You'll need to manually capture payment within the authorized period. If you set up manual capture, you will have to capture payments from the Orders page in your admin."*

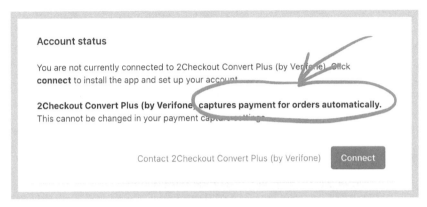

Account status

You are not currently connected to 2Checkout Convert Plus (by Verifone). Click **connect** to install the app and set up your account.

2Checkout Convert Plus (by Verifone) captures payment for orders automatically. This cannot be changed in your payment capture settings.

Contact 2Checkout Convert Plus (by Verifone)   Connect

[1.4.24b]

Authorized Period

There is one caveat to manually capturing payments:

All credit card payment providers have an authorized period to allow a charge to be made to a customer's credit card. The authorization process first checks that the credit card is valid, and then that the card has enough funds on it for the transaction.

The authorized period will end after a certain amount of time. The length of the authorized period depends on your credit card payment provider. You need to capture a payment within the authorized period to collect money for your order.

Shopify Payments provides an authorized period of 7 days.

NOTE: *When you process the payment, the fraud and risk checks activate.*

> Pro CAUTIONARY Tip: When a large order is activated in your store, and it is typically not your average transaction amount, be suspicious and do some due diligence to check if it is fraudulent. A good practice is to email or call your customer and verify that the order/credit card is legitimate. Most customers will appreciate your diligence in protecting their credit cards. The risk of not checking is that the order will be shipped, the credit card owner refutes the charge, and you don't have your products or money!

NOTE: *If you have this choice activated, you will be reminded in the orders and also notifications from Shopify to fulfill your orders and capture payments.*

Step 2. Add your choice

The choice will show in the payment dashboard.

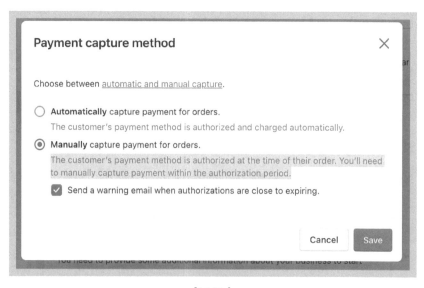

[1.4.24c]

YOUR SHOPIFY STORE PAYOUTS (MONEY)

**Where to find this in Shopify? Finances > Payouts*

Each payment must be processed when you set up a payment provider to accept credit card payments. Therefore, there is usually a delay between when the customer pays for their order and you receiving the payment. After the payment is processed, the purchase amount will be transferred to your merchant account (which you have designated in your Shopify Payment section).

Other payment providers, such as PayPal, will have ways of getting funds from your customer to a holding account. You will have to transfer funds manually from your PayPal account.

NOTE: Check with the service you are using to find out how they will pay you.

If you are using Shopify Payments, you can check your pay period to see when you'll receive payouts from credit card orders. Other payment providers have their own rules about when you receive payouts for credit card orders. Check with your provider to figure out how often you will be paid.

After the payout is sent, your bank might not receive it immediately. It can take a few days after the payout is sent for it to be deposited into your bank account. The deposit timing depends on your bank and its system. Check with your bank if you find your payouts are being delayed.

There are 2 ways to see your Shopify Payments payouts.

**Settings > Payments > View Payouts

[1.4.48]

OR

**Finances > Payouts

[1.4.49]

💡 Pro Tip: Remember, banks are closed
Saturdays, Sundays, and Holidays.
Processing will not occur on these days.

THE FINANCIAL PROCESS FROM END-TO-END

**Where to find this in Shopify? Finances > Overview*

You can get your financial overview of Shopify Payment payouts, fees, and billing.

> Pro Tip: Shopify payouts are payments from customer orders. Shopify fees relate to your Shopify plan, credit card, shipping, and app fees.

[1.40.50]

Do you understand how your money moves between payment providers, credit card issuers, and banks?

In this next section, I have gathered information from banks, credit card companies, and Wikipedia. I have added the resources at the end of the chapter, but I have tried to create excellent comprehensive information for you. I will show you how the whole financial process works between your Store, the credit card company, and the banks so you have some knowledge of how money moves around.

How A Credit Card Payment Gets Processed

When a customer pays for an online order using a credit card, the payment must be processed before the funds are added to your merchant account. Credit card processing is done for you by your payment provider, in this case, Shopify Payments.

Fees

If you have Shopify Payments enabled, you won't be charged transaction fees for any orders made on your online store. Instead, you'll pay a card rate (discount rate) which depends on your Shopify plan. If you use a third-party payment provider with Shopify, then Shopify will also charge you a fee for each transaction.

> Pro Tip: You can avoid transaction fees by activating Shopify Payments, Shopify's payment provider.

Generally, you can be charged several transaction fees for online transactions. The issuer, the acquirer, and the credit card company all charge a small fee for using their services for credit card transactions.

A quick overview of fees that you might be charged:

- *Processing/discount rate*
- *Authorization fees*
- *Transaction fees*
- *Return fees*
- *Address verification (AVS) fees, and gateway fees*
- *Per item fees*
- *Communication fees*
- *Wireless fees*

You will always pay a processing fee (2.9%, 2.4%, etc.) when you initiate a credit card transaction. This is also called a Discount rate or just rate.

You will also pay an authorization fee (.10, .15, .30, etc.), depending on volume and payment provider.

The rest of the transaction fees depend on the payment provider you choose. Shopify does not always provide a Shopify Payment option in different countries. You will have to use a third-party payment provider. Shop around to get the best rate and fees and check the small print.

HOW YOUR MONEY MOVES

The Customer: Your customer is the person that makes a purchase with their credit card from your Shopify store in 'Checkout'.

Payment Provider or Processor: The payment provider in Shopify are either Shopify Payments or third-party Payment Providers.

The Payment Terminal: The payment terminal is your Shopify store or the Shopify Point-of-Sale system connected to your Shopify store.

The Merchant: Shopify Payments or a third-party Payment Provider is the merchant that provides several functions to the Shopify store. First, they register their business with the various card networks so they can accept all the payment types required. Shopify Payments or a third-party Payment Provider also arranges for the processed funds to be deposited back to the Shopify store, typically within a few business days. Shopify Payments or a third-party Payment Provider provides the Shopify store with the equipment, software or platform needed for them to accept credit cards.

The Issuer: Your customer's credit card financial institution - The issuer is the bank that underwrites, extends the credit, and backs the card/credit extended on behalf of the Card Network. The issuer is the bank of the customer.

The Acquirer: The bank or a financial institution that processes credit or debit card payments on behalf of Shopify Payments or a third-party Payment Provider. The acquirer allows Shopify stores to accept credit card payments from the card-issuing banks within an association.

Credit Card Network: Credit card networks (Visa, MasterCard, Discover. Etc.) are the bridge between all the various elements that comprise a transaction, from the customer all the way through to funding. They ensure the authorization and funds movement are properly directed to ensure money is appropriately distributed.

The Payment Process

The payment process has four stages:

1. *Authorization*
2. *Capture*
3. *Clearing*
4. *Funding*

Authorization

- *Your Customer uses their credit card.*
- *Shopify Payments or a third-party Payment Provider requests authorization from the customer's bank.*
- *The customer's bank authorizes or denies the transaction.*
- *Shopify Payments or a third-party Payment Provider sends the transaction details to the Credit Card Network.*
- *The Credit Card Network sends the transaction details to the customer's bank.*

- *The customer's bank validates the transaction, sends an Approval Code or denies the transaction.*
- *The Credit Card Network notifies Shopify Payments or a third-party Payment Provider whether the transaction is approved or not.*

Capture

After the payment is authorized, the payment must be captured in the Shopify store. When a payment is captured, details about the payment are sent to the acquirer.

The Shopify store displays the approval message in your Shopify Admin > Orders.

Clearing

- *The Acquirer reviews the payment details.*
- *The Acquirer requests the necessary funds from the issuer.*
- *The Issuer processes the customer's credit card.*
- *The Credit Card Network sends the transaction information to the Issuer.*
- *The Issuer subtracts their fee.*
- *The Issuer sends the remaining amount to the Credit Card Network.*
- *The Credit Card Network subtracts their fee.*
- *The Credit Card Network sends the remaining amount to the Acquirer.*

Funding

- *The Acquirer subtracts their fee.*
- *The Acquirer transfers the final amount to the Merchant.*

What's amazing about the above is that most transactions go
through these steps in less than a second, providing real-time
authorizations to merchants across the world. Visa alone processes
thousands of transactions per second across its network, serving
over 150 million transactions between cardholders and merchants
worldwide every day.

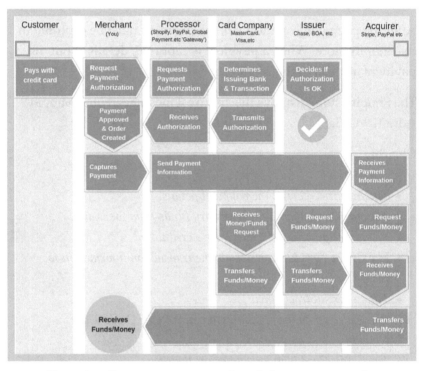

Illustration of how your money moves through the payment process by
Veronica Jeans

How Often Do You Get Paid?

If you are using Shopify Payments, then you can check your pay
period to see when you'll receive payouts from credit card orders.
Other payment providers have their own rules on when you
receive payouts for credit card orders. Check with your provider to
figure out how often you will be paid.

After the payout is sent, it can take a few days after the payout is sent for it to be deposited into your bank account. This depends on your bank and its system. Check with your bank if you find your payouts are being delayed.

> Pro Tip: Remember, banks are closed Saturday, Sunday, and Holiday. Processing will not occur on these days.

RESOURCES:

Here is a link to my TOOLS page: **https://veronicajeans.online/resources**

Here is a resource on the Shopify support page.

Activating PayPal. **https://veronicajeans.online/shopify-paypal**

Manual Payments **https://veronicajeans.online/shopify-manual-pay**

Helcim **https://veronicajeans.online/helcim**

Acquiring bank **https://veronicajeans.online/wiki-bank**

https://veronicajeans.online/creditcard

Read more about GDPR: **https://eugdpr.org**

Restricted Shopify Payment Products: **https://help.shopify.com/en/manual/markets/markets-pro/prohibited-items**

CHAPTER 5
CHECKOUT & ACCOUNTS

****WHERE *to find this in Shopify? Settings > CheckOut &*
*Accounts***

The checkout process is part of the customer journey in your store,
and you want to make it as seamless as possible for your customers
and at the same time, obtain enough information to ship the
purchased products.

What to Expect in This Chapter:

- *Customize style*
- *Customer accounts*
- *Customer account URLs*
- *Customer contact method*
- *Customer information*
- *Tipping*
- *Order processing*
- *Marketing options*
- *Abandoned checkout emails*
- *Order status page*
- *Checkout language*

[1.5.1]

CUSTOMIZE STYLE

You can choose what your checkout form (which is your checkout page) will look like by adding color, background images, etc.

When you click the 'Customize checkout' you will be pushed to the Theme editor.

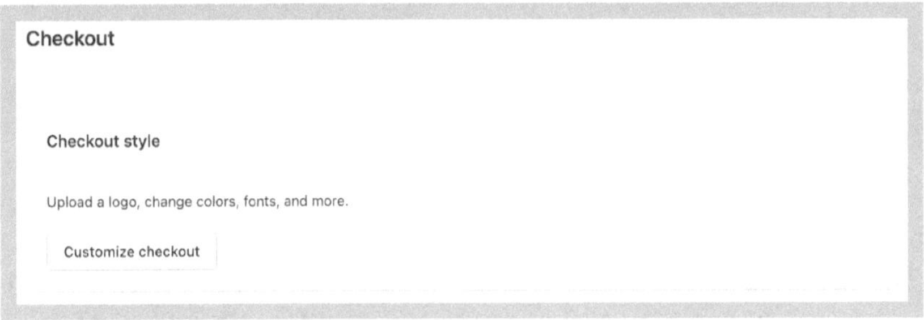

[1.5.2]

NOTE: *We have not prepared you for branding and customizing your store yet. All the information about branding and customizing your checkout in book 2 in the chapter about setting up your Theme.*

This chapter is about information to set up Checkout for your customers.

CUSTOMER ACCOUNTS

There are 2 options for your customers:

- *Allow customers to log in from the online store and checkout*
- *Require customers to log in before checkout*

Don't make this option a requirement unless you want customers to create an account before buying your products. This obstructs customers from buying from you and will affect your sales.

[1.5.3]

The first option - allow customers to log in - will give customers an option to either log in with their account or check out as guests.

[1.5.4]

You can have both options available in your online store. But if you do, your customers with a 'new customer account' will have to retrieve their digital code from the email forwarded to their email address - every single time they buy something!

[1.5.4a]

If your customers create an account, they can view their orders in the account created for them. When a customer logs in, the details stored in their account are auto-filled during checkout for a faster checkout experience.

The customer account gives your customer the option of a refund or to return items if required only if you have activated the new customer accounts option. This is not available to all Shopify stores.

[1.5.5]

Customers can either check out normally or with their customer account.

I believe in giving your customers a choice and not forcing them to create an account.

CUSTOMER ACCOUNT URLS

You can control how customers log in with different customer accounts.

Give customers access to log in to your online store by sending the URLs directly or adding them to your store navigation.

[1.5.7]

New customer accounts

New customer accounts let your customers log in using an email and a one-time 6-digit verification code. A password isn't required to log in.

When customers log in for the first time, the account is created automatically for them.

Classic customer accounts

You can use URLs (website addresses) if you want to give them to customers or add them to your navigation (menu).

Customer account URLs

Give customers access to log in to your online store by sending the URLs directly or adding them to your store navigation.

New customer accounts   Preview

https://kalaharigold.account.myshopify.com

Customers will log in with a one-time code sent to their email.

Classic customer accounts   Preview

https://kalaharigold.com/account/login

Customers will log in with email and password.

[1.5.6]

Multipass for classic customer accounts

Enable Multipass if you want to integrate with an external customer account system

You can only enable Multipass if you have a Shopify+ account.

CUSTOMER CONTACT METHOD

Customers can use their phone or email to check out to receive order and shipping notifications:

Phone

The customer's email might not be collected using this method. Customers who choose to get shipping and order information through SMS might not leave an email address. It is a good idea to give your customers an option.

Some information about SMS:

- *There is no charge to you for text messages.*

- *A customer cannot reply to the SMS notification.*
- *It is not possible to end an abandoned cart message.*
- *Customers will not receive an email and SMS notification. They choose which one they want.*
- *You can turn off SMS notifications in individual customer orders.*

Email

Collecting your customer's email is very important for contacting them for reviews, remarketing, etc., once they have bought products.

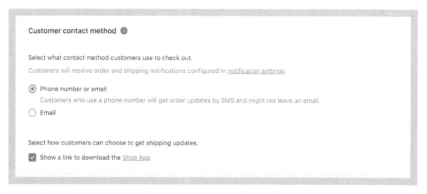

[1.5.8]

Check the 'Show a link to download the 'Shop App' - this is another way for customers to get their orders and shipping information via email.

CUSTOMER INFORMATION

Do not forget to change the option in this section. I have changed the options to give you the maximum advantage in gathering your customers' information at checkout.

- *Full name: A good reason to require first and last names is that you can address the customer invoice with the full name and personalize your subsequent emails.*
- *Company name: If you do business with other businesses, schools, etc. (B2B), leave the company 'optional'. If you are doing business directly with customers (B2C), you can keep the 'Company name' requirement hidden.*

- ***Company Address:*** *Address line 1 is automatically added to your checkout form. Keep the 'Address line 2' optional for more shipping information if customers have apartments or additional address requirements. Do not make this a 'Required' option.*
- ***Shipping address phone number:*** *Give your customers the option to choose to add their 'Shipping address phone number'. As I have said before, giving your customers choices is a great idea.*

Form options
Choose whether your checkout form requires extra information from your customer.

Full name
○ Require last name only
◉ Require first and last name

Company name
○ Hidden
◉ Optional
○ Required

Address line 2 (apartment, unit, etc.)
○ Hidden
◉ Optional
○ Required

Shipping address phone number
○ Hidden
◉ Optional
○ Required

[1.5.9]

TIPPING

This is a new option in Shopify. I suggest only using this option if your customer is used to tipping in your industry.

Tipping

Include the option for customers to add a tip at checkout. Learn more about tipping ↗ .

☐ Show tipping options at checkout

Customers can add a tip to their online purchase and show their support for your business.

[1.5.10]

ORDER PROCESSING

While the customer is checking out:

When your customers enter their shipping or billing addresses, they can be presented with address suggestions from Google Autocomplete. This feature lets your customers enter their address information faster and more accurately. These address suggestions come from Google, not from your customer's browser. If this feature is disabled or your customers live in a country where it isn't supported yet, then your customers can check out as usual by entering their addresses manually.

Order processing

Change how your store responds to checkout and order events. Learn about order processing ↗ .

While the customer is checking out

☑ Use the shipping address as the billing address by default

Reduces the number of fields required to check out. The billing address can still be edited.

☑ Enable address autocompletion

Gives customers address suggestions when they enter their shipping and billing address.

After an order has been paid

○ Automatically fulfill the order's line items

◉ Automatically fulfill only the **gift cards** of the order

○ Do not automatically fulfill any of the order's line items

After an order has been fulfilled and paid

☑ Automatically archive the order

Fulfilled orders will be automatically removed from the open orders list.

[1.5.11]

After an order has been paid

You have these options:

- **Automatic Fulfillment of Orders:** Choose this option if you don't have any products available for pre-order, you're selling digital downloads, or you're using a fulfillment service. I would not automatically fulfill orders because of the high-risk of fraud, but it is your choice. You can choose not to fulfill any orders automatically.
- **Manually fulfilling orders:** *Manually fulfilling orders lets you easily keep track of your inventory and control when an order is sent. Manually fulfilling orders might be the best order fulfillment method if one of the following situations applies to your business:*
- *You make products to order,*
- *You have products available for pre-order,*
- *You sometimes run out of stock and want to be able to easily offer your customers partial fulfillment without having to issue a refund.*

Your automatic order email will be sent as soon as you fulfill the order.

After an order has been fulfilled and paid, or when all items have been refunded

You have one option to check:

- **Automatically archive the order:** My suggestion is to automatically archive your order; it makes your life easier —one less thing to think about when you are fulfilling your orders. When you choose this option, the order will be removed from your list of open orders, but not from the order dashboard. The order will still be visible on your dashboard.

MARKETING OPTIONS

Your customer can sign up for marketing. You want to take advantage of the signup choice.

[1.5.12]

Checking the pre-select option is against the General Data Protection Regulation (GDPR) rules. The GDPR is about giving your customers a choice to sign up but to opt-out of your marketing emails.

GDPR affects your European customers. Even if you are only selling to USA customers, Europeans who live in the USA temporarily or visit could buy from you. If they order from you, they are still under GDPR protection.

So, it is up to you to choose if you are a USA Shopify store owner.

Customize checkbox labels

You can change the language or text for the checkbox labels to suit your brand and voice.

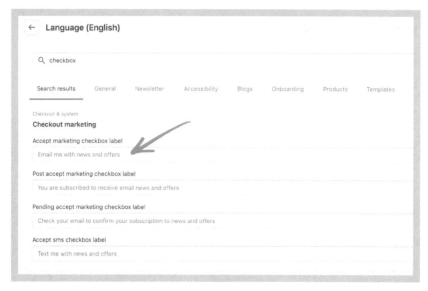

[1.5.13]

NOTE: To collect SMS consent, you need to set up terms of service and privacy policy in your legal settings. We will cover the setup of all the Policies in Chapter 17.

ABANDONED CHECKOUT EMAILS

You will lose about 68% of your customers to 'abandoned checkouts.' This means that while they are checking out, there are several reasons why they don't complete the step. For example, they get interrupted, look for their credit card, and get sidetracked by the kids, they cannot decide. There are varied reasons. Using the automatic 'abandoned checkout' email notification is a great way to remind prospective buyers that they can still decide to buy.

You can recover 10% - 50% of sales using 'abandoned checkout' emails.

Abandoned checkout emails ⓘ   Customize email
Send an email to customers who didn't finish checking out.

> ⓘ A new abandoned checkout automation is available. The new version features improved email editing and workflow
>   customization. To view this automation, visit marketing automations.

☑ Send abandoned checkout emails automatically

Send to
◉ Anyone who abandons their checkout
◯ Email subscribers who abandon their checkout

Send after
◯ 1 hour
◯ 6 hours
◉ 10 hours (recommended)
◯ 24 hours

[1.5.14]

Send abandoned checkout emails automatically

Check this box to send the abandoned cart emails automatically.
The first email will be sent out but if you want a sequence of emails,
then you can automate some more emails in the setting
'Marketing.' There are 2 options.

- *Email subscribers who abandon their checkout.*
- *Email anyone who abandons their checkout*

The second choice is the best because you want to target those
customers that have abandoned their checkout and not just your
existing email subscribers.

Send timing

Testing the time limit you send the email after your prospective buyer has left your store is a great idea. Shopify recommends 10 hours, but you might decide to send it sooner or later.

Abandoned checkout notifications and email sequences is covered in-depth in my series Shopify Made Easy book 3, 'Optimization Your Shopify Store - 2023'.

ORDER STATUS

In this box you can add customization using scripts or code. I only suggest this is for experienced web developers.

[1.5.15]

This is a great place to:

- *Add conversion tracking for your order status page*
- *Show content when a particular shipping method is used*
- *Show content based on customers' locations*
- *Add a message to your order status page using Javascript.*

Here is a link to some examples: https://veronicajeans.on-line/customize-orders

CHECKOUT LANGUAGE

This is a way to change the headers or language for your checkout. I would not change the language unless you know some phrases that would work better to get more conversions.

Checkout language

Your store's checkout page is displayed in **English**

Manage checkout language

[1.5.16]

I suggest that you view the checkout pages of other brands for different types of language / text. Most of the time, the language for the checkout is standard, and customers are used to the same language.

RESOURCES:

Here is a link to my TOOLS page: **https://veronicajeans.online/ resources**

Order status page examples: **https://help.shopify.com/en/manual/ orders/status-tracking/customize-order-status**

CHAPTER 6
LOCATIONS FOR SHIPPING

WHERE *to find this in Shopify? Settings > Locations*

First, we set up your locations before implementing the 'Shipping and delivery' settings. Unless your locations are set up properly, your shipping information will not function correctly, affecting the delivery of your products.

What to Expect in This Chapter:

- *Locations*
- *Default Location*
- *Location Priority*
- *Multiple locations*

Your locations in Shopify are the physical location that you are shipping your products from, whether they are your own products or products from a drop shipper or manufacturer.

This information will be how your checkout and orders will calculate the shipping costs for your customer. The customer will see this address on the packing slip and the shipping label.

LOCATIONS

[1.6.1]

NOTE: *You cannot use a Post Office Box as a shipping address.*

Shopify automatically uses the physical business address you added to 'Store Details' as your shipping location. If you are shipping from your business address, verify it.

If you are shipping from a separate location or drop shipping, you can change the location setting. Once you have established your shipping location, delivery details, such as shipping rates, can be recalculated.

[1.6.2]

If your Post Office Box address was automatically added as your shipping address, create a new location for shipping.

The maximum number of locations that you can have depends on your plan:

- *Shopify Starter - 2*
- *Shopify Lite - 3*
- *Basic Shopify - 4*
- *Shopify - 5*
- *Advanced Shopify - 8*
- *Shopify Plus - 250*

Step 1. Add or change locations

Click on the 'Manage' button on the top right side of the dashboard.

Add a short name to make the location easy to identify. These locations will be in either your shipping, orders, or products. Your customers will not see the location titles.

Check the box to fulfill online orders from this location if this is your shipping address.

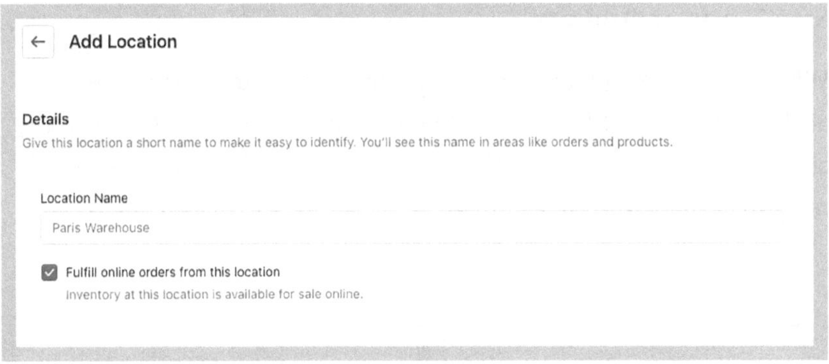

← **Add Location**

Details

Give this location a short name to make it easy to identify. You'll see this name in areas like orders and products.

Location Name

Paris Warehouse

☑ Fulfill online orders from this location

Inventory at this location is available for sale online.

[1.6.5]

Step 2. Add an Address

When you create a location, the system will try to verify your address. If your address cannot be verified, you will get a warning, as in the following image. This means USPS/UPS/FedEx doesn't recognize the shipping address.

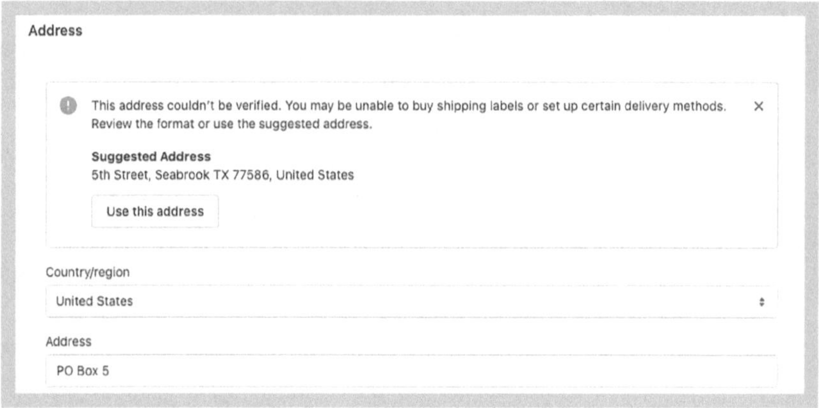

Address

This address couldn't be verified. You may be unable to buy shipping labels or set up certain delivery methods.   ×
Review the format or use the suggested address.

Suggested Address
5th Street, Seabrook TX 77586, United States

Use this address

Country/region

United States

Address

PO Box 5

[1.6.6]

As I mentioned before, it cannot be a Post Office Box address. It must be a physical address.

When adding the address, Google will verify your address with a dropdown of various addresses.

Country/region

United States   ⇕

Address

1900 shipyard

1900 Shipyard Drive, Seabrook, TX, USA

1900 Shipyard Boulevard, Wilmington, NC, USA

1900 Shipyard Road, Chesapeake, VA, USA

1900 Shipyard Road, Shenandoah, VA, USA

1900 Shipyard Road, Manns Harbor, NC, USA

Powered by Google

[1.6.7]

Step 3. Deactivate a Location

If you have specified a wrong location address in this section,
deactivate the location and save it. Then you can delete the location
you do not want to use. It keeps it nice and tidy.

When you deactivate a location, it will not count toward your
location limits in your plan.

You can't deactivate a location associated with a private or third-
party app. Instead, remove the app.

You cannot deactivate your default location. Allocate another
location as the default before deactivating the location.

A location has to be deactivated before you can delete a location.

Step 4. View Inventory

Once the products have been added to your store, you can now
allocate inventory to your products.

This will be covered in the chapter on Products.

Step 5. Shipping from multiple locations

You need to activate multi-origin shipping if you are shipping products from multiple locations.

Consider activating multi-origin shipping if you run your store in the following ways:

- *You have multiple retail locations or places where you fulfill orders.*
- *You ship online orders from one or more locations, which can include fulfillment service locations.*

The multi-origin shipping is activated to all new Shopify stores by default. If you can't create a shipping profile in your Shipping and delivery settings, then your store is using single-origin shipping.

After you activate multi-origin shipping, your order fulfillment can be split between locations. If you have more than one active location that fulfills online orders, then your orders are split for fulfillment in the checkout based on product inventory levels.

When the products in an order are in different shipping profiles or need to be shipped from different locations, a shipping or delivery fee is calculated for each item and then all the shipping fees are added together. The customer is shown only the final shipping cost at checkout

> Pro Tip: You do not need to add multiple locations when you start your Shopify store. You can add it anytime.

DEFAULT LOCATION

Step 1. Change default location

The address added to your 'Store Details' is automatically allocated as your default location.

In the section 'Default location', click on 'Change default location' to view your locations.

Select a location in the drop-down to change the default setting and save.

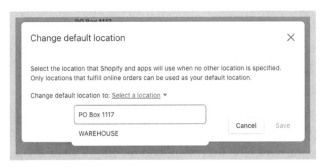

[1.6.3]

Here are some tips for the locations:

- *The default location is also allocated automatically to your products and apps. Only physical products can be allocated to a location.*
- *You can allocate location settings for your products in the products, shipping, or delivery settings.*
- *If you use apps to stock inventory, then the apps will be allocated as a location. Inventory apps include drop shipping, third-party logistics, and custom fulfillment services.*

The drop shipping apps Printful and Subliminator are App locations shown in the following image. The POD or drop shipping apps will automatically add their locations in the location settings.

[1.6.4]

LOCATION PRIORITY

Step 1. Allocate priority location

If you want to allocate a priority location - orders will ship from the location which is on the top of the list. Click on 'View or edit location priority.'

[1.6.12]

Step 2. Move a location

To move a location, put your cursor on the square dots (6 dots), hold it down, and drag the location where you need it when the cursor hand shows.

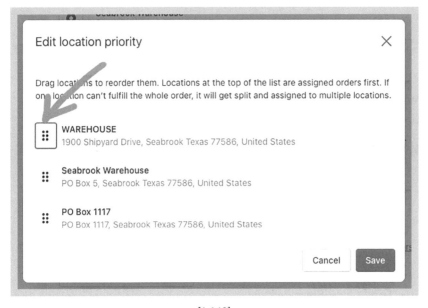

[1.6.13]

Locations at the top of the list are assigned to orders first. If one location can't fulfill the order, it will get split and assigned to multiple locations unless you have allocated the location at the product level.

CHAPTER 7
SHIPPING & DELIVERY

WHERE *to find this in Shopify? Settings > Shipping & Delivery*

Your choices of shipping services are either Shopify shipping services (USPS, UPS, DHL Express) or your shipping accounts (FedEx, USPS, UPS, DHL).

What to Expect in This Chapter:

- *Shipping Rates Overview*
- *General Shipping Rates*
- *Custom Shipping Rates*
- *Processing Time*
- *Local Delivery*
- *Local Or In-Store Pickup*
- *Packages*
- *Shipping labels*
- *Packing slips*
- *Carrier accounts*
- *Custom order fulfillment*

You can choose which states in the USA you want to deliver to and which countries you wish to ship to internationally.

If you have never dealt with shipping internationally and are located in the USA, I suggest that you start shipping in the USA only. If you are an international business, start your business in your own country before going outside the borders.

SHIPPING RATES OVERVIEW

When you start selling and shipping your products, you will probably have to adjust your shipping/weights/prices. They are determined by the customers buying your products. For instance, if your products are heavy or are of different dimensions, the handling percentages will either have to be included, or you might have to increase your prices. It is not always easy to set up your shipping correctly. Once you are established, it is much easier if you are confident shipping locally to expand to ship internationally. Shipping internationally has many hurdles to overcome.

Shipping rates are what you charge your customer and the cost of the products they order. The cost of any shipping rates is added to a customer's order at checkout. There are different types of rates to ship your packages:

- *Custom Flat Rate: Flat rate shipping means the shipping price is not connected to the weight, shape, or size of the shipped item, hence the term "flat rate." The shipping rates will be set up manually, and you determine the price and/or weight breaks between the different rates.*
- *Calculated Rate: Third-party shipping carriers or services determine the calculated shipping rates. These would include USPS, UPS, or DHL Express for domestic shipping within the USA and USPS, UPS, and DHL for international shipping. You*

choose which shipping carrier you want to use and which will benefit your customers with the best and cheapest shipping rate.

- **Mark-Up or Discounted Rate**: *If you use calculated shipping rates, you can add a 'Handling Fee', which will create higher or lower shipping rates for your products, i.e. bulky or heavy products.*
- **Free Shipping Rate**: *You can create free shipping on all of your products, some of your products, or free shipping over a specific value.*

Choose where you ship and how much you charge for shipping at checkout. To charge different rates for certain products, create a shipping profile.

Shipping profiles

Shipping profiles help you charge accurate shipping rates through product-based shipping rules. You can use shipping profiles to set shipping rates for specific products and charge different amounts based on where you're shipping your products to and from. You can add products that should share shipping rates to a shipping profile, and then set up shipping zones and rates for each location that fulfills those products.

There are two ways to create a shipping profile:

- *General Shipping Rates*
- *Custom Shipping Rates*

GENERAL SHIPPING RATES

Where to find this in Shopify? Settings > Shipping & Delivery > General Shipping

In this section, shipping zones and rates are set up for all products in your Shopify store. There are no different rates for different products. This section includes domestic and international shipping zones.

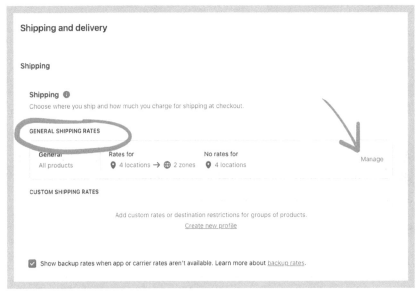

[1.6.19]

Step 1. Manage general shipping rates

Set up shipping in your Shopify store for all your products. You will see 'Products' and '0' in the first section if you have not added any products yet, but the products will be automatically allocated to the 'General Shipping Rates.'

You will see your products displayed if you have added products to your Shopify store.

[1.6.26]

As we have no products added to your store yet, '0' products will show in this section. As you add your products, they will automatically be added to the default location.

Step 2. Set your location

The first step is to set the location you will be 'Shipping from.'

If the address shown is the correct address, that is great. You don't have to change anything.

[1.6.21]

Remove a location if it is not relevant to your product shipping location.

The following image shows that your products can ship from different locations in the same zone. The different locations are allocated in the product information page section.

[1.6.22]

Pro Tip: You can also add different products to the same or different locations and create a custom shipping profile. See how when we show you how to set up custom shipping profiles.

Domestic Shipping Zones

Step 3. Change shipping zone and rates

Shopify automatically created a series of flat shipping rates in the shipping zone. If you do not want to use the flat rates, delete the zone as shown to be able to set up your new shipping rates.

[1.6.23]

If you have a USA store, your shipping information will show the local zone (in this case, USA) and rates that Shopify automatically added. These are random weights and shipping rates.

If you have an international Shopify store, your 'Domestic' zone would be the country you are doing business in. Shopify automatically added a free shipping rate with no added conditions.

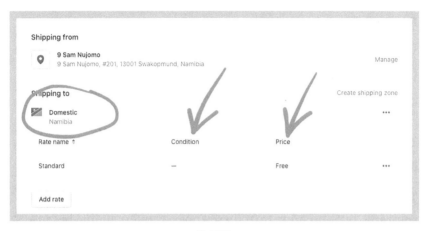

[1.6.24]

Step 4. Add your domestic shipping zones

A shipping zone is a country you will be shipping from.

In this section, create your Domestic shipping zones. You can name these zones anything you want to. The customer does not see the names. I would name them according to the zone you chose to set up, i.e. 'Domestic' or 'Local.'

In this example, we will set up the 'Domestic zone' in the USA. If you are in a different country, you will set up your 'Domestic zone' for your country. Select 'Create shipping zone' on the right; the country options will open, and you can choose your country.

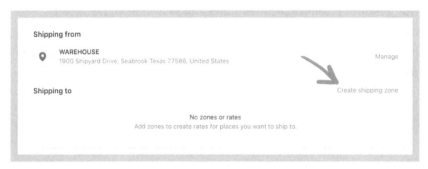

[1.6.25]

Domestic Zone in the USA

You choose where you want to ship to. There are 62 locations in the USA zone that you can ship to. These include the normal 50 States, the USA territories listed below, and Washington DC (which is not classed as a state).

Some USA states are very expensive to ship to and need some extra information.

The territories are not classed as international but rather domestic shipping. But you must treat these zones as international because you must fill out import/export forms to ship to the territories. This might be more trouble than it is worth. You make the decision.

Here are locations in the USA zone which need more paperwork:

- *American Samoa*
- *Federated States of Micronesia*
- *Guam*
- *Marshall Islands*
- *Northern Mariana Islands*
- *Palau*
- *Puerto Rico*
- *U.S. Virgin Islands*
- *Armed Forces Americas, Europe, Pacific*

Suggestion: *I would start with states and Washington, DC before considering the USA territories. Get comfortable shipping your products, and then decide if you need to venture out more. It really depends on where your customers are.*

Pro Tip: Make sure you know what the cost of your product is and what it costs to ship it. If you want to add FREE shipping to your store, you need to add that cost to your product cost. Also, don't forget to consider your variable and your fixed costs!

Domestic Zone for other countries (international)

When you add your address in 'Store details', the country you registered is automatically added to your local shipping zone.

Create a local zone for the country of your business and where you are shipping from, as shown in the following image.

[1.6.27]

Step 5. Set up your domestic shipping rates

Every zone needs the shipping rates added. Otherwise, customers won't be able to check out if they live in this zone.

Select 'Add Rate', and a new window will open.

[1.6.28]

You have 3 choices for shipping rates.

- *Set up your own rate*
- *Use carrier or app to calculate rates*
- *Set up FREE shipping*

METHOD 1. SET UP YOUR OWN RATE - CUSTOM FLAT RATE

Flat rate shipping means the shipping price is not connected to the weight, shape, or size of the shipped item, hence the term "flat rate." The shipping rates will be set up manually, and you determine the price and/or weight breaks between the different rates.

[1.6.15]

When to use flat shipping rates?

Shipping methods that require flat rates include:

- *Free shipping In-store pickup*
- *Various regular postage rates*
- *Deliveries managed by a fulfillment service.*

There are three types of flat shipping rates:

- **Weight-based rates** – *set your shipping rates based on the total weight of the orders you receive.*
- **Price-based rates** – *set your shipping rates based on the price of the orders you receive.*
- **Free shipping**

In the following image, each step shows how to set up your own rates.

[1.6.29]

Step 1. Choose a name for your shipping option.

Customers will see this name at checkout. Make it a recognizable name that customers are used to which always has to do with transit or shipping time.

Step 2. Add your price for this shipping option.

Research existing shipping prices for your shipping rate, so you don't lose money. Be aware that shipping prices change frequently, and you will need to update these prices manually.

Step 3. Choose the shipping option.

There are two options for shipping rates:

- **Weight-based Shipping:** *Weight-based rates are usually more accurate than price-based rates because they reflect the actual* *costs of shipping a customer's order. Weight-based rates include the combined weight of the products in the order, the weight of any inserts, and the weight of the packaging.*

- ***Price-based Shipping:*** *Basing your shipping rates on prices of your products can be inaccurate because the products will have different weights unless all your products are the same weight. All price-based shipping rates are calculated based on discounted totals. If a customer uses a discount code, shipping for the order is calculated based on the discounted order total.*

Step 4. Choose the minimum option for the shipping price

For each manual or flat rate level, you need to set the minimum option – weight or price. For instance, the first shipping rate is the minimum weight of '0' for $6.00.

Step 5. Choose the maximum options for the shipping price.

Then the maximum weight for $6.00 will be 1pound. Each rate has its own weight and price. If you set the price levels, it is the same. Although setting a rate for a price might be a little more difficult, because shipping worldwide is based on weight and not price because it can vary so much.

METHOD 2. USE CARRIER OR APP TO CALCULATE RATES - REAL-TIME SHIPPING

Calculated shipping rates are the automatic rates you choose by the shipping carrier. These default carriers include USPS, UPS, or DHL Express for domestic shipping within the USA.

DHL, UPS, and USPS shipping carriers are available with your Basic Shopify Plan. You must upgrade to integrate FedEx as one of your shipping carriers.

The number of shipping carriers that are available to you depends on where your business is located and whether your Shopify subscription plan has the carrier-calculated shipping feature.

Countries that are integrated with Shopify by default are:

- *United States*
- *Canada*
- *United Kingdom*
- *Australia*
- *France*

If your shipping carrier is not available on the list of default services, you might have to add a Shopify App to provide calculated rates.

The integrated shipping carriers have a discounted rate for Shopify merchants depending on your country.

Step 1. Choose a shipping carrier.

You choose which shipping carrier you want to use and which will benefit your customers with the best and cheapest shipping rate.

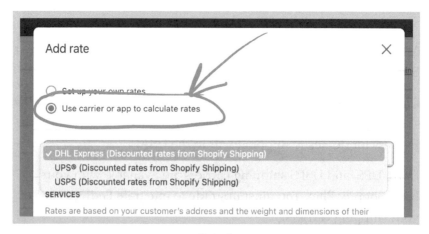

[1.6.16]

If you add UPS as a shipping carrier, Shopify will automatically ask you to create a UPS account when you save this shipping carrier. You must register and answer some questions to create an account.

[1.6.40]

Step 2. Choose a type of shipping service

Check all the shipping services you want to add. Rates are based on your customer's address and the weight and dimensions of their order.

SERVICES

Rates are based on your customer's address and the weight and dimensions of their order.

☐ UPS 2nd Day Air A.M.® (commercial addresses only)
☐ UPS 2nd Day Air®
☐ UPS 3 Day Select®
☐ UPS Next Day Air Saver®
☐ UPS Next Day Air®
☐ UPS Next Day Air® Early
☐ UPS Worldwide Expedited®
☐ UPS Worldwide Express Plus®
☐ UPS Worldwide Express®
☐ UPS Worldwide Saver®
☐ UPS® Ground
☐ UPS® Standard

[1.6.30]

Pro Tip: Do not try to add them all because it is really confusing for your customer. At this stage you don't want to do that, because they are ready to get out their credit card and buy your product.

Step 3. Choose to update new shipping services

The rates will be updated automatically when they change. The rates for the different shipping services can increase randomly. You might miss the notice, which could cost you money because you are not charging your customer enough for shipping fees.

FUTURE SERVICES

☐ Automatically show new shipping services to customers when they become available

[1.6.31]

Step 4. Add a handling fee if appropriate.

In this section, you can increase or decrease your shipping rates to add a handling fee. There are various reasons for adding this option.

[1.6.17]

For example, if the rate is too high to attract customers, you could discount it by a certain percentage to increase sales. If the rate is too low to cover your packaging and handling costs, you can increase it.

Here is another reason to add a markup. If you have large or bulky lightweight items, the calculated shipping rates would not reflect your actual shipping rate because shipping is calculated by dimensional weight which is the height, width and length by the weight. So if the shipping rate is by weight, checkout prices will not reflect how much it actually costs you to ship.

You can markup calculated shipping rates by an additional flat fee or by a percentage of the total shipping rate. If you adjust a calculated shipping rate to include an additional flat fee and a percentage markup, then the percentage is calculated before the flat fee is added. For example, a $5.00 rate with a 50% markup and a $1.00 flat fee costs the customer $8.50, not $9.00.

If you want to offer discounted shipping, then enter a negative value. For example, -5% or -$2.50."

> Pro Tip: Test some products and see how much the shipping rates are and how much the label would cost in a test order.

METHOD 3. SET UP FREE SHIPPING

You can create free shipping on all of your products, some of your products, or free shipping over a specific value.

> Pro Tip: If you offer FREE shipping, consider adding the cost to your prices. I advise that when calculating your product prices, add the free shipping costs to your initial price. Or if you are offering FREE shipping, create an offer of, for instance, free shipping over $150 (which depends on your product prices).

Consumers tend to want to avoid shipping costs and will spend more to avoid shipping costs.

[1.6.18]

Step 1. Set your free shipping rate.

Free shipping is set up with 'Set up your own rate.' because we do not need to use calculated shipping rates.

Step 2. Name your shipping rate

Name your rate FREE SHIPPING - remember the name will be visible to your customers.

Step 3. Set your price for your rate

Your price is obviously $0 (it is free).

Step 4. Set your conditions

- *Price-Based Free Shipping: Example: Buy $150 and get free shipping. Your minimum price would be $150 and no maximum price.*

- *Weight-Based Free Shipping: Example: Free shipping over or under a certain weight.*
- *Free Shipping on all products: Suppose you have free shipping on ALL your products. No minimum and no maximum weights or prices. Set up under Price-Based Shipping.*

Step 5. Set your minimum weight and maximum weight.

Don't forget your Box/Letter/Package weight, including the weight of any inserts in your package. For example, if you wanted to offer free shipping on orders only above $50, then you would set the Minimum order price to $50. Alternatively, if you want to offer free shipping for orders that contain four or more products, you can make each product weigh 1 pound and then create a free shipping rate with the 'Minimum order weight' set to 4 pounds.

INTERNATIONAL ZONE & RATES

If you do not want to ship internationally, your customer will be informed that there is no shipping internationally, or shipping to their specific country.

> Pro Tip: Start with local shipping/domestic shipping and get familiar with your shipping process before broadening your horizons.

But, if you feel confident to ship internationally, here is what you need to set up.

Step 1. Decide which countries you want to set up for shipping.

Check the appropriate country where you want to ship your products.

The following image shows the international shipping zone under the 'General profile' settings.

In the three dots on the right of the 'Rest of the word' section, you will be able to add the specific country where you want to sell your products.

[1.6.33]

Shopify has automatically added fixed prices for shipping. This is just a suggestion and is not necessarily the correct shipping cost.

[1.6.34]

Step 2. Add the different countries

Once the window opens, add the different countries. Shopify has added the rest of the world, which is probably not a good idea. Everybody thinks they want to be available to anybody that wants to buy. But realistically, you will not sell to other countries unless you have either marketed to those countries or your product is unavailable in that particular country.

[1.6.35]

You can set up each country separately or add several countries in the same zone.

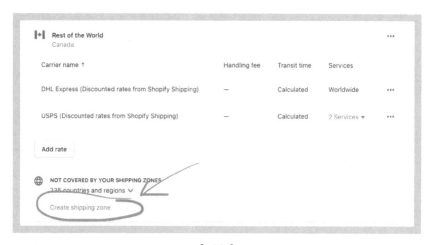

[1.6.36]

All your chosen countries will be shown as seen in the following image.

[1.6.37]

Step 3. Add your shipping rate.

You have two choices for your rates.

- *Set Up Your Own Rate (Manual Shipping Rates*
- *Calculated Shipping Rates*

> Pro Tip: I have not added FREE shipping for the international zone, because it would be prohibitive to add that to your costs. But it is your decision, as with everything in your store.

Follow the steps set out in the Domestic shipping zone.

If your local country is not the USA, and you add the USA as another country, there will be no available carriers. Remember you are shipping out of the local country TO the USA and will have to have your local shipping carrier, which is not integrated by default into Shopify. No carrier options will be available if you don't have default carrier rates in a particular country.

Add rate   ×

○ Set up your own rates

◉ Use carrier or app to calculate rates

There are no carriers or apps available for this zone.

Cancel   Done

[1.6.38]

Check out Shipping Apps to add to your Shopify store to get real-calculated shipping prices. It is not always an option; you will have to add your own shipping prices per product weight to your store.

> Pro Tip: If you ship internationally, I suggest adding a note to your shipping information about the VAT, Taxes, and Duties. (This can be found under the setting - Legal pages).

CUSTOM SHIPPING RATES

**Where to find this in Shopify? Settings > Shipping & Delivery > Custom Shipping*

You need to create a new profile if you want to charge different rates for only certain products.

[1.6.20]

Shipping profiles help you charge accurate shipping rates through product-based shipping rules. For example, if you are shipping from different locations for a specific product, you need to create a profile for each product-specific shipping rate and zone. The shipping rates will be different for each profile.

First example: Suppose you have different shipping rates for different products. For instance, you want to create flat-rate shipping for some products and calculate shipping for others.

Second example: One set of products will only be shipped in the USA. Another set of products can be shipped to the USA and

Canada. And a few can be shipped to the USA and Internationally. So, you have 3 different customer shipping rate profiles!

When the products in an order have different shipping profiles or need to be shipped from different locations, a shipping or delivery fee is calculated for each item and then all the shipping fees are added together. The customer is shown only the final shipping cost at checkout.

Step 1. Activate multi-origin shipping

If you have an existing Shopify store, you might still be on the single-origin shipping option in Shopify. If this is a new Shopify store, the multi-origin shipping is set up by default, and there is nothing extra to do.

After you activate multi-origin shipping, your order fulfillment can be split between locations. If you have more than one active location that fulfills online orders, then your orders are split for fulfillment in the checkout based on product inventory levels.

Step 2. Add a name for your profile.

Make your profile name very logical - for instance, 'Domestic & Canada'. In this sample, domestic shipping will be the USA, and Canada is the only international zone.

Add your products to the profile that suits your shipping requirements.

[1.6.24]

Step 3. Create a shipping zone

On the same page, create a Shipping Zone (at the bottom of the page) for the USA (your domestic shipping zone), and you will get a pop-up. Once you have added your choice, click Done.

[1.6.25]

Step 4. Add your flat rate or calculated rate to your zone.

The information and actions are the same as for all the other different zones.

If you have more custom profiles, rinse, and repeat.

PROCESSING TIME

**Where to find this in Shopify? Settings > Shipping & Delivery > Processing

Adding an estimated delivery date to your store can increase your conversion in your store. Here are several requirements and considerations to add processing time to your store:

- *Delivery dates are only available in certain countries depending on which shipping rate type you set up*
- *Delivery dates don't work with shipping rates provided by third-party apps.*
- *If you're using negotiated carrier-calculated shipping rates with Canada Post or UPS, then some mail services might not support delivery dates.*
- *Delivery dates don't work with negotiated FedEx-calculated rates.*
- *If your checkout shows a mix of eligible and ineligible shipping rates, then delivery dates aren't displayed for your eligible rates.*

Show delivery dates to your customers by setting a processing time if you process orders in 2 business days or less. This will be added to the transit time of your shipping rates. This option will add delivery dates for your customers the same as Amazon adds to checkout.

Processing time   Inactive

Show delivery dates to your customers by setting a processing time, if you process orders in 2 business days or less. This will be added to the transit time of your shipping rates. Learn more about processing time.

Manage

[1.6.44]

Step 1. Add a processing option to your store.

Until you add this option to your store, this will be inactive.

Step 2. Check 'Use processing time to show delivery dates at checkout.'

How long does it take to process an order, from when it is placed to when the package is handed to the carrier? This will be added to the transit time of the carrier.

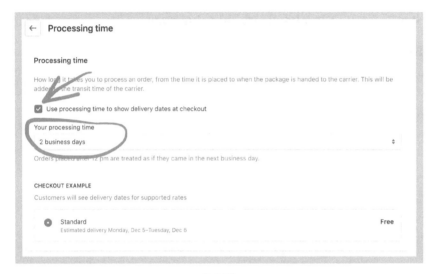

[1.6.45]

The choices are the following:

- *Same business day*
- *Next business day*
- *2 Business days*

Orders placed after 12 pm are treated as if they came in the next business day.

LOCAL DELIVERY

Where to find this in Shopify? *Settings > Shipping & Delivery > Local delivery*

You can set a delivery area by mile radius or ZIP code. Depending on how far you want to travel to deliver your products. If you are delivering locally,

Step 1. Create a local delivery shipping zone

To create a local delivery shipping zone, decide which location you are going to be delivering in.

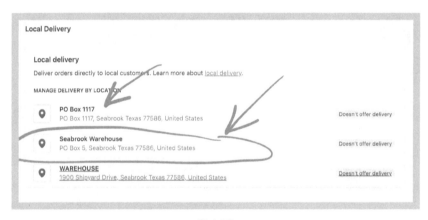

[1.6.43]

Remember, a PO Box location cannot be used as a location to deliver locally from.

Step 2. Manage delivery by location

Click on the address or location you want to activate as your local delivery location. Once you click, this screen will appear.

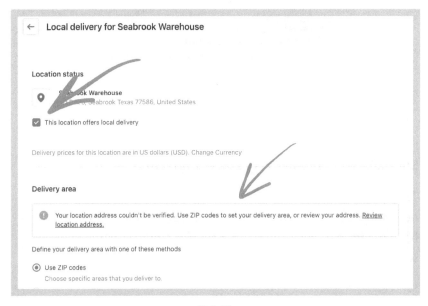

[1.6.47]

If the address of your location cannot be verified, you will need to fix that in 'Locations.'

Step 3. Define delivery area

Choose the delivery zone by zip code or distance radius of the delivery area. You can also include neighboring states or regions. Add the distance measurement - either km or m (miles).

[1.6.48]

> ⸱ Pro Tip: Ensure you know your costs for local delivery. Remember, it is time and money that you are spending to deliver locally. If you become very busy, you might have to get a courier service. A great idea is to get a quote from courier services so you are prepared.

Step 4. Define your delivery zone information

This information will be visible to the customer. Here you can add a note and define several delivery zones for your local delivery. As I have mentioned, get rates from a courier service to give an idea of what you should charge.

DELIVERY ZONE   •••

Zone name

Local Delivery   14/50

Delivery radius up to

99.0   mi

Minimum order price   Delivery price

$ 0.00 $ 50.00

Add conditional pricing

Delivery information

DELIVERY ONLY IN THE HOUSTON AREA. If you are more than 45 miles from Webster, contact us to make arrangements. Delivery is within 3 Days. Contact us if you need your sculpture sooner.
info@artisticafrica.com

IF YOU ARE OUT OF STATE:
Contact Us!

246/255

This message will appear at checkout and in the order confirmation notification.

[1.6.49]

If you only want to do local free shipping, you need to name your shipping zone very clearly. Not that it will stop buyers who are not local from using the free option. For some reason, buyers never read the information.

Add a note to your offer, which will appear in checkout and the order confirmation.

The note should include, for instance, how long it would take to process the order and other delivery information. This message will be sent out in your local order confirmation notification (email).

Also, you can add conditional pricing - e.g., Orders from $0.00 up to (or no limit) and the delivery prices. Or add more conditional pricing.

[1.6.50]

Step 5. View your 'checkout preview'.

> Pro Tip: Always think of the future – If you are doing the local delivery, what if you added an extra employee to help you, what would you have to charge to cover the rates? Or if you involve a courier service.

Step 6. Add more zones with a different delivery prices.

You can create multiple local delivery rates within a province or state by specifying the delivery region in the shipping rate's title. For example, Local delivery - Houston or Free Toronto delivery for postal codes starting with M4, M5, M6, and M8. Of course, any customer within the province or state can still select this option, so if a customer outside your intended region chooses the method, you'll need to contact the customer.

. . .

Step 7. Change local delivery zone information

If you want to change the information in any of the zones, click on the location address or the link 'Offers delivery' to make changes.

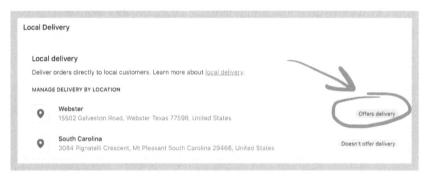

[1.6.51]

LOCAL OR IN-STORE PICKUP

**Where to find this in Shopify? Settings > Shipping & Delivery > Local or in-store pickup

You can offer customers an option to pick up their orders. This is mainly for retail store owners or if you have a business address for your eCommerce store. This is not a good idea if you work from home.

> Pro Tip: Some of my customers use a local retail store for deliveries.

You can set up the option for customers to pick up their online orders at your retail store, curbside, or any location you choose. To do this, enable the local pickup option for each location where customers can go to get their orders.

Step 1. Choose your locations for local pickup.

Click on the address or the link 'Doesn't offer delivery.'

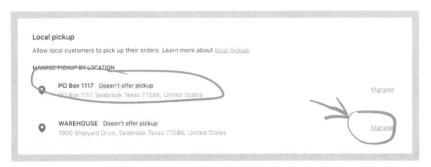

[1.6.52]

The same as before, you cannot do a local pickup from a PO Box number.

Step 2. Location offers local pickup

Check the box 'Location offers local pickup' because no information is available for you to add unless you check the box.

[1.6.53]

Step 3. Information at Checkout

All pickup pricing is free. There is no choice. Add expected pickup time to what suits your business.

Information at checkout

Expected pickup time

Usually ready in 24 hours

CHECKOUT PREVIEW

⬤ WAREHOUSE   Free
       1900 Shipyard Drive, Seabrook Texas 77586, United States   Usually ready in 24 hours

Location name and address shown at checkout are set in location settings ↗

[1.6.54]

Step 4. Order ready for pickup notification

Add a note for the customer to tell them what to do when arriving at your store. The note will give your customer more information about the location name and address shown at checkout, whatever is set in your 'Locations.' Then, add our own little spin to the message.

Order ready for pickup notification

Pickup instructions

Bring your confirmation email when you come to collect your order.

                                             66/255

If you're offering curbside pickup, you can let customers know what to do when they arrive at your store.

[1.6.55]

PACKAGES

Where to find this in Shopify? Settings > Shipping & Delivery > Packages

You need to select a package type that matches the type of order you're fulfilling. Until you add a package, Shopify will use a sample box to calculate shipping rates at checkout. Each package will show the accurate shipping rates at checkout

The shipping rate price will be automatically calculated at checkout by adding the package weight to your product weight. Do not add the package weight to your product weight.

Add the weight of the extra packaging materials you are adding with your product, which will determine the total weight of your product and package. This will influence the weight of the shipping price. For instance, a card, tissue paper. Make sure you add all your extra marketing materials etc., to the weight of the package.

Step 1. 'Add package' for your products.

[1.6.56]

You have a choice - 'Custom packaging' or 'Carrier packaging'.

- *Custom Packaging: If you have your own packaging or get your packaging from a vendor other than a shipping service. Then you can choose from Box, Envelope, or Soft package or satchel.*
- *Carrier Packaging: Packaging from a Shopify-approved shipping service, only UPS or USPS. You can get free packaging from the default shipping services/carriers. However, you will probably have to create an account with each carrier.*

[1.6.57]

Carrier packing from USPS or UPS are only the general packaging available. If you have different sizes you need to add them to your 'Custom package'.

[1.6.58]

Step 2. Add the dimensions of your package

If you are adding custom packaging, add the dimensions for the package (L x W x H), which are the units of measurement, and don't forget to add the weight of the box. The weight of the package will be automatically included in your product weight to give you an accurate weight for your shipping cost at checkout. Don't forget to add the weight of your internal packaging, cards, invoice, etc.

The package sizes you use to ship your products. Weight and dimensions of the default pac

Edit Sample box package ✕

Name

Sample box

Length	Width	Height		Weight when empty (optional)
8.6	5.4	1.6	in	0.5	lb

Cancel   Save

[1.6.60]

Step 3. Choose your package size.

You will be provided with all the shipping carrier's types and sizes of packaging. Add all the different types and sizes you will use for different shipping situations.

> Pro Tip: A suggestion is to do some research in what size package you will need for your products. Also, find out how many products you can get into a package to minimize the cost of shipping.

Step 4. Set your default package

Set the package that you use the most as your default package. You cannot allocate a different package to each product (yet). Set your most used package as your default.

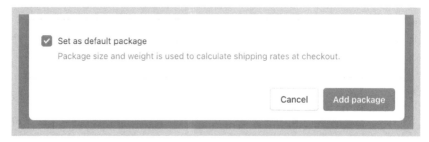

[1.6.59]

SHIPPING LABELS

Where to find this in Shopify? Settings > Shipping & Delivery > Shipping labels

Shipping labels are attached to the outside of a shipping package. The labels show information that shipping carriers use to ensure a shipment is delivered correctly. Most labels contain the following pieces of information:

- *Recipient's name, address, and phone number - This lets the carrier know where to deliver the shipment and provides a way to contact the recipient if necessary.*
- *The sender's address lets the carrier know where to return the shipment if it can't be delivered to the recipient's address.*

Every label has a barcode, which is how the carrier tracks the shipment's progress. Shipping labels can also include the following information:

- *The shipment's order number*
- *A tracking number*
- *The date when the order was shipped*
- *The type of shipping service that was purchased*
- *The shipping carrier's information*

Before you ship your packages, you must purchase a shipping label and attach it to your shipment's packaging.

Depending on how your business is set up, either you or your supplier purchases shipping labels. Generally, whoever is giving the shipment to the shipping carrier is the one who purchases the shipping label. If your supplier purchases the label for the shipment, then they usually charge you for the cost.

Shopify Shipping

If you have a USA or Canadian store, Shopify offers discounted shipping labels from carriers, which include the shipping prices. Or you can print your own shipping label with our own shipping carriers.

You can get reduced shipping rates from USPS, DHL Express, UPS, or Canada Post. After you've bought a shipping label, you can print it, fix it to the outside of your package, and then ship it from any post office, UPS store, or location.

The post office or the UPS store will not charge you for this service.

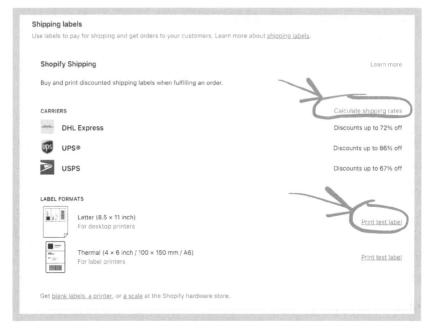

[1.6.61]

Shopify also provides shipping insurance if you buy the labels through your Shopify store. You add the insurance per order once you create a shipping label in 'Orders.'

Step 1. Calculate shipping and label formats

You can calculate how much you'll save when you buy discounted labels from Shopify Shipping. You can either use a pre-cut and sticky shipping label or print the shipping information on plain paper. If you are using a sheet of paper, use the plastic cover that the carrier service will be able to supply and make sure to stick it down very thoroughly so that it cannot be ripped off during shipping.

HINT: *More sticky tape is always better! Although using plain paper is not advisable.*

Shopify does supply labels and printers on their website.

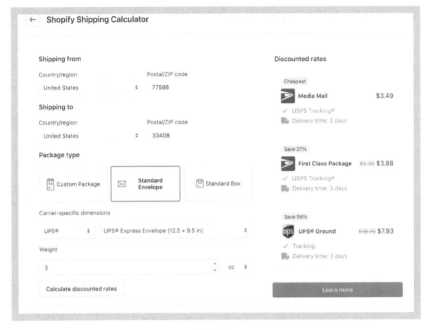

[1.6.62]

Step 2. Connect your printer to your PC or laptop.

Test print your shipping labels to make sure you like how it prints and it prints correctly on your label or paper. This is the place to set up your label printer for the correct size to print your labels. If you don't have a label printer, then it does not matter.

[1.6.66]

Step 3. Print labels with orders

When you receive an order, you choose and print your label in the 'Orders' section.

[1.6.63]

The default package you allocate in this section will determine the shipping cost in checkout. You can check out the different shipping rates for each package and compare prices.

PACKAGE AND WEIGHT

Package   Add package

CUSTON TEST PACKAGE   Default
12 × 15 × 6 in, 5.5 oz

Total weight (with package)

2.3438   lb

SELECTED BY CUSTOMER

Media Mail $4.83 USD

[1.6.64]

You can also add a different package to the order, which will change the shipping costs for the order. Once you have the package allocated to the order, all you need to do is decide what day it is shipping and if you want your customer to be emailed with the shipping information for their order

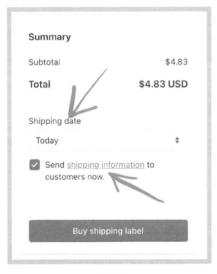

[1.6.65]

.

PACKING SLIPS

**Where to find this in Shopify? Settings > Shipping & Delivery >
Packages Slips*

Step 1. Edit packing slip template

Packing slips

A printed list of items in a shipment that often goes inside a package.

Packing slip template   Edit

Customize the packing slips you can print when you're fulfilling orders.

[1.6.67]

You may not want to use this feature unless you want to add a
personal note or additional information to your packaging slip.
Adding a personal message or extra information is probably a good
idea to stand out from your competition. If you do not know
coding, ask an expert for help. You can add something to the
bottom of the coding without expertise, but it might look out of
line.

Step 2. Preview packing slip

You can preview the packing slip. It is always a great idea to check
your changes.

[1.6.68]

The following image show what the packing slip looks like.

[1.6.69]

CARRIER ACCOUNTS

Where to find this in Shopify? Settings > Shipping & Delivery > Carrier accounts

Step 1. Enable third-party calculated rates at checkout

You might need to upgrade your plan to enable calculated shipping rates using accounts from FedEx, UPS®, Canada Post and apps.

Step 2. Connect and manage account

Connect and manage external shipping carriers and fulfillment services. Add the shipping services here if you have your own shipping carrier account and negotiated shipping rates.

[1.6.70]

CUSTOM ORDER FULFILLMENT

Where to find this in Shopify? Settings > Shipping & Delivery > Custom order fulfillment

Step 1. Add your custom fulfillment center email address.

Your customer order fulfillment center will be emailed every time you get an order. You can only add ONE fulfillment center / zone in this section. If you have different vendors, you will have to use an App.

NOTE: When you mark an item or complete order as fulfilled in your Shopify admin, the fulfillment service is sent an email with all the order information so that they can fulfill it for you.

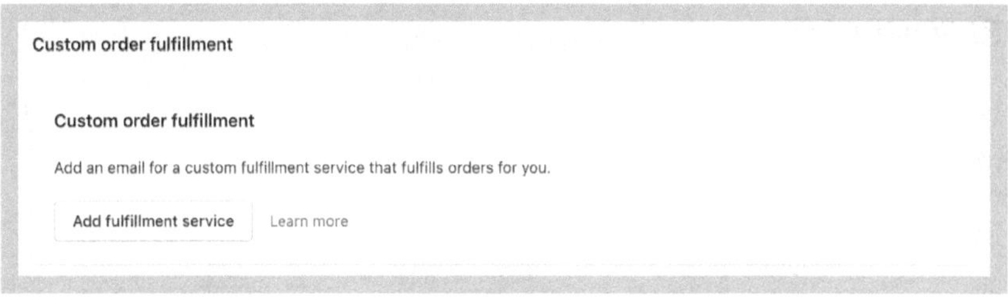

Custom order fulfillment

Custom order fulfillment

Add an email for a custom fulfillment service that fulfills orders for you.

Add fulfillment service   Learn more

[1.6.73]

RESOURCES:

Shipping App for International shipping and local freight transport in the USA:

InXpress - DHL at Checkout

https://veronicajeans.online/shopify-dhl

DHL Carrier Rating for the US and Canada-based merchants Only.

I use InXpress for my LTL in the USA and international shipping. Contact seth.kornfeld@inxpress.com for more information.

Naming your own rates:

https://veronicajeans.online/shopify-rates

Manual Shipping rates

https://veronicajeans.online/shopify-manual

Third-Party Carriers

https://veronicajeans.online/shopify-carriers

Shipping Strategies

https://veronicajeans.online/shopify-ship

Packaging

https://get.packhelp.com/shopify

Here is the bottom line about shipping... If you are just starting, stick to the basics, and make your shipping as simple as possible.

I have given you enough information to set up your basic shipping and provide some tips and links for you to check out on Shopify Help. They have excellent detailed information.

Here is a link to my RESOURCES & TOOLS page:

https://veronicajeans.online/resources

CHAPTER 8
TAXES & DUTIES

**WHERE *to find this in Shopify? Settings > Taxes and duties*

As an eCommerce business, you might have to charge taxes on your sales and remit the taxes to your government.

You can use Shopify to automate charging taxes, but Shopify does not remit or file your taxes. Taxes calculated in your Shopify store are SALES, GST, or VAT taxes and not income tax (earnings).

What to Expect in This Chapter:

- *Taxes & Duties*
- *Set Up Sales Tax Collection*
- *Manage Tax Collection*
- *Tax Rates and Exemptions*
- *Tax Reports*
- *Duties and Import Taxes*
- *How Tax is Charged*
- *European Union VAT*
- *Tax-exempt Customers*

There is so much information for different countries and USA states, that it is an impossible task in this chapter. The questions I have tackled are ones that some of my new clients had problems with. Research as much as possible for your situation.

It's your responsibility to consult with local tax authorities or a tax professional to verify that you charge your customers the correct tax rates and to ensure that you file and remit your taxes correctly.

The following guide is for setting up your tax information in Shopify and any reference or advice is for informational purposes only and is not intended to replace professional tax advice.

TAXES & DUTIES

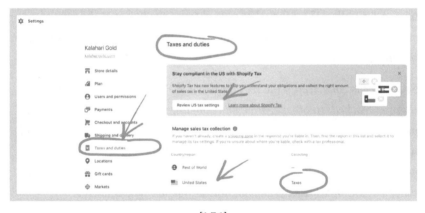

[1.7.1]

If you are selling products, you are responsible for collecting taxes. First, let's define the types of taxes.

INCOME TAX

Income tax is the amount you pay on your total income from the business minus the sales tax and business expenses to the federal and state, or government, depending on your state in the USA or your country. One common misconception is that online sellers don't have to file income tax unless they make above a certain amount of money per year or unless they receive a distribution from the business. The tax authority in any country wants you to pay tax on every penny of income you receive.

SALES TAX, VALUE-ADDED TAX (VAT), OR GOODS AND SERVICES TAX (GST)

These taxes are a percentage your customers have to pay when they purchase certain items from your business. It is determined by each state or country.

Note: *in the USA, with limited exceptions, it is not the federal government that charges sales taxes, but the states.*

Thomson Reuters says: *"Both sales tax and VAT are types of indirect tax – a tax collected by the seller who charges the buyer at the time of purchase and then pays or remits the tax to the government on behalf of the buyer.*

Sales tax is collected by the retailer when the final sale in the supply chain is reached. In other words, end consumers pay sales tax when they purchase goods or services. When buying supplies or materials that will be resold, businesses can issue resale certificates to sellers and are not liable for sales tax. Until the sale is made to the final consumer, sales tax is not collected, and tax jurisdictions do not receive tax revenue.

VAT, on the other hand, is collected by all sellers in each stage of the supply chain. Suppliers, manufacturers, distributors, and retailers all collect VAT on taxable sales. Similarly, suppliers, manufacturers, distributors, retailers, and end consumers all pay VAT on their purchases. Businesses must track and document the VAT they pay on purchases to receive a credit for the VAT paid on their tax return. Under a VAT regime, tax jurisdictions receive tax revenue throughout the entire supply chain, not just at the point of sale to the final consumer. https://tax.thomson-reuters.com/en

HOW TO KNOW WHERE TO PAY TAXES

> Pro Tip: I suggest starting doing business in your own country and, once you are comfortable selling & shipping, then expand your market.

There are two criteria:

- *The buyer pays the sales tax if they reside in the same state or country your business has a presence in (presence can mean manufacturing, offices, warehouse, etc., in any location). For example, if your business is in Texas, but your warehouse is in New York, your obligation to collect taxes will be in both states.*
- *The buyer pays sales tax where the product is shipped to. This comes under the threshold rule for different states in the USA, whether you are a USA-based company or an international company. While the buyer has a legal burden of paying the tax when they purchase a product, the seller (you) is responsible for collecting the tax and handing over the collected tax to the county, state, or country.*

In most countries, there is a threshold before you are responsible for paying taxes.

In the USA, a 2018 Supreme Court decision, South Dakota vs. Wayfair, determined that each state sets its own rules for out-of-state sales. Many states give a break to businesses with less than $100,000 in sales or a certain number of transactions, but some have rules even for small businesses.

The threshold rule does not count in the state or country where your business is. You will most likely always have to collect taxes, depending on the state or country.

Research your government or state website to find out what the regulations are.

For instance, the information on the Comptroller.texas.gov website: **"Texas sellers must collect sales tax on taxable items, including shipping and delivery charges, sold online in Texas**. Texas sellers are engaged in business if they have a physical Texas location or make online sales in Texas."

Quote from our Sales Tax Yogi - Amy Monroe: *"State Tax regulations are changing in the United States, and the regulation is different in every state according to what Dollar ($) amount you are selling or the number of units you are selling. For instance, if your business is not domiciled in a state, you might be liable for the Sales tax if you sell 200 units or sell over $100k products."*

Check with a sales tax expert or tax firm that deals in state taxes in the USA (a CPA might not know this information).

NOTE: *If you are an international eCommerce business selling to United States customers, you are responsible for state taxes, depending on each ruling for each state.*

SHOPIFY & TAXES

Starting January 3, 2023, only Shopify Tax will be updated with new features. The Basic Tax and Manual Tax services will continue to work and receive tax rate updates, but they won't receive new features. Review the following table to determine which tax service is best for your needs:

https://help.shopify.com/en/manual/taxes/us/choose-tax-service

Choose your tax service   ✕

You have free access to Shopify Tax for the rest of 2022 and for your first $100,000 in US online sales per calendar year after that. Choose which tax service to use **starting January 3, 2023.** Learn more about each option.

⦿ Continue with **Shopify Tax**   Recommended

◯ Switch to **Basic Tax**

Choose if you want to be notified about other options.

☐ **Manual Tax** (available January 3, 2023)

☐ **Third-party tax options** (coming 2023)

                                        Cancel   Save

[1.7.4]

If different tax regions are registered in Shopify, and you are not registered in that state or country, you can remove the regions not needed.

We will work through all the sections so you know your Shopify store is set up correctly to collect taxes.

If you are new to eCommerce, research to determine if you must charge tax before you begin selling.

Your business address will automatically calculate your tax region, including the municipal taxes. If you have an office in one state and your inventory is in another, Shopify will calculate both state taxes. You must add both addresses to charge the tax obligations in your Shopify store.

SET UP SALES TAX COLLECTION

The types of products that are taxed depend on if the product is physical or digital and the laws in the state in the USA or your country.

For instance, the information for digital products on the Comptroller.texas.gov website says: *"Texas law applies sales tax to digital goods if the items would be taxable if delivered in physical form. Digital products, such as photographs and music are tangible personal property as defined in Section 151.009 of the Texas Tax Code."*

It may be necessary for you to register with various tax agencies. You can set up your taxes in Shopify to ensure you charge the correct rates wherever you sell.

With Shopify, you have location-based or registration-based tax calculations. Taxes may be registration-based or location-based in Shopify.

In the United States, the sales tax you should charge can be affected by several factors:

- *The location your product is shipped from.*
- *The location your product is shipped to.*
- *Where you're registered to collect tax.*
- *Item taxability Buyer exemptions.*

> Pro Tip: If you haven't already, create a shipping zone in the region(s) for which you're liable. Then, find the region in this list and select it to manage its tax settings. If you're unsure about where you're liable, check with a tax professional.

Registration-Based Tax

Registration-based taxes require you to input a tax registration number to automatically calculate the taxes. This means you must get your business's sales tax permit from your local tax authority. Registration-based taxes in Shopify are only for the following countries:

- *United States*
- *Canada*
- *European Union*
- *United Kingdom*
- *Norway*
- *Switzerland*
- *Australia*
- *New Zealand*

Location-Based Tax

If you are not based in the countries mentioned above and need to charge taxes, then the taxes are applied at the country or regional level, depending on the tax laws.

Step 1. Determine your sales tax obligations

Click on the country registered in your Shopify store or 'Review US tax settings.' Both will get you to the same section on the dashboard.

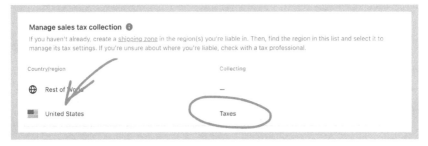

[1.7.9]

Step 2. Determine your current tax service

Check out the tax services that Shopify has added to your store.
Click on 'Manage.'

[1.7.3]

Step 3. Manage tax service

Here you can choose different tax services. Shopify has
automatically added the Shopify Tax package.

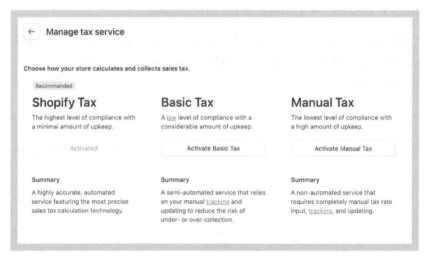

[1.7.3a]

When setting up your taxes for the United States, you can choose the tax service that works best for your business. You can select Shopify Tax, Basic Tax, or Manual Tax to calculate and collect taxes from your customers at checkout. You can change which tax service you use at any time.

Here is a list of benefits with the new Shopify tax system:

- *Registration-based tax collection*
- *Taxes are automatically collected for states where you have a registered tax liability.*
- *Rate calculation using product categories*
- *Tax exemptions and modifications are calculated automatically based on the category of the product.*
- *Automatic recommendations for product categories Product categories are automatically suggested for your products.*
- *Rooftop accuracy calculates taxes precisely according to street address, rather than being limited to zip codes. This feature is only included in Shopify Tax.*
- *Support for state fees. Some states collect tax-like fees. For example, in Colorado, orders containing taxable goods that are delivered by a motor vehicle in Colorado are subject to a $0.27 non-refundable retail delivery fee. This feature is included only in Shopify Tax.*
- *Tax holidays, special tax rates that apply on specific dates are automatically calculated. For example, Texas has a sales tax holiday from August 5-7 each year. This feature is only included in Shopify Tax.*
- *Shopify Markets Pro option makes it easier to sell to a new international market. Only Basic Tax or Shopify Tax support Markets Pro. You can't use Manual tax with Markets Pro.*
- *Tax reports enables you to access reports that show the amount of taxes you've collected.*

- *Liability insights are automatic suggestions and insights on your potential liabilities are provided based on where you ship and sell to.*
- *Advanced tax reports have additional details about the amount of tax you collect, and can be used to help you file with tax authorities.*
- *B2B tax exemptions enable you to sell licensed products that are tax-exempt.*
- *Customer tax exemptions enable you to designate that specific customers are tax-exempt.*
- *Product and shipping tax overrides apply specific tax rates that override any other tax calculations for selected products or shipping destinations. Overrides can only be applied at the state level for Manual Tax.*
- *Collecting tax in states with no state sales tax enables you to collect tax in states that have no overall tax rate. For example, if you're in New Hampshire and you sell prepared and consumed on-site food, then you might need to apply a 9% tax rate.*

When setting up your taxes for the United States, you can choose the best tax service for your business. You can select Shopify Tax, Basic Tax, or Manual Tax to calculate and collect taxes from your customers at checkout. You can change which tax service you use at any time.

Step 4. Third-party tax options

Check the box to get automatic third-party tax options.

Third-party tax options

Shopify will launch other tax options in 2023.

☑ Notify me when new tax options are available

[1.7.3b]

MANAGE TAX COLLECTIONS

Now let's get to where and how you need to collect taxes.

For USA-based companies, Shopify has a 2023 tax-based offer:

"Collect the most accurate sales tax rates with precise, address-based calculations and product categorization. It's free for the rest of the year and then free for your first $100,000 in US online sales per calendar year."

Step 1. Verify your taxes per region

The tax is based on where the product is **delivered**. Verify which country you are going to ship your products from.

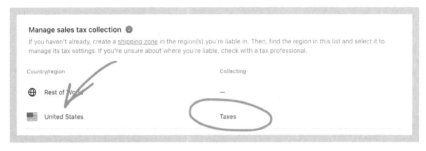

[1.7.9]

Step 2. Fill out your registered tax permit in Shopify

Click on the three dots on the right side of the region you collect taxes.

[1.7.11]

Step 3. Add tax information

Enter the number you were issued by your regional tax office.

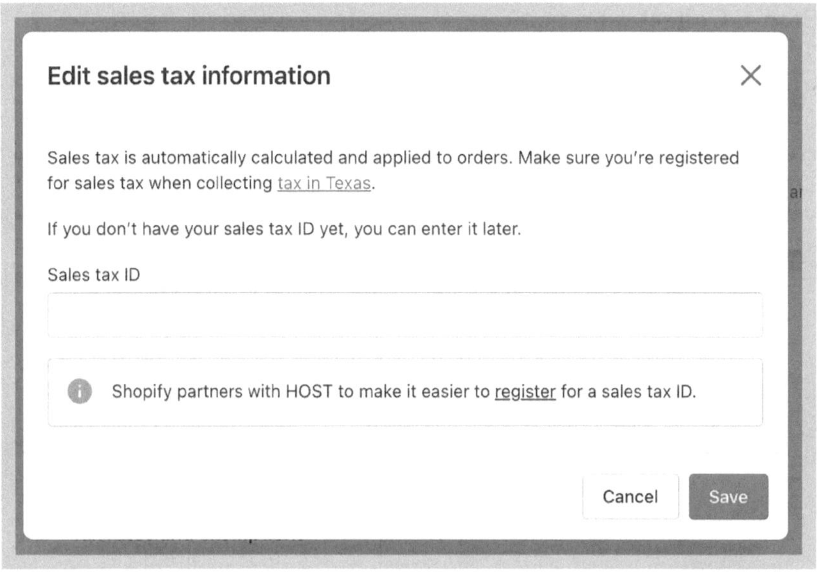

Edit sales tax information   ✕

Sales tax is automatically calculated and applied to orders. Make sure you're registered
for sales tax when collecting tax in Texas.

If you don't have your sales tax ID yet, you can enter it later.

Sales tax ID

ⓘ   Shopify partners with HOST to make it easier to register for a sales tax ID.

                                                  Cancel   Save

[1.7.12]

As you can see in the following image, the location-based tax only has one tax percentage added. If it is different to what Shopify has added, change it here. If you have an office in one state and your inventory is in another, you must calculate both state taxes.

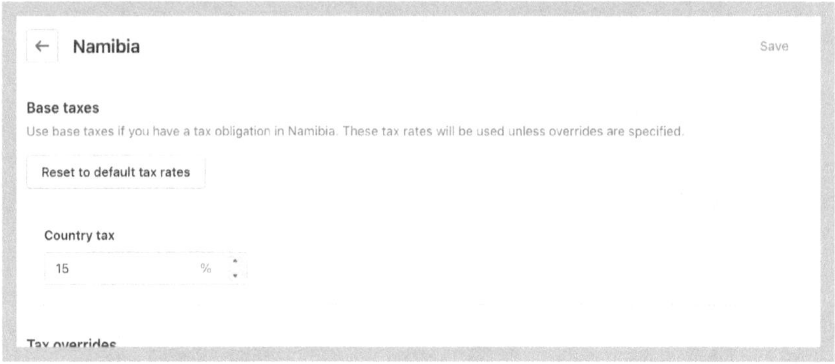

←   Namibia   Save

Base taxes
Use base taxes if you have a tax obligation in Namibia. These tax rates will be used unless overrides are specified.

Reset to default tax rates

Country tax

15   %

Tax overrides

[1.7.13]

Step 4. Collect sales tax

Click on 'Collect sales tax.'

[1.7.14]

Allocate the state where you must collect tax and your tax permit number.

[1.7.15]

Check the resources at the chapter's end to research your required tax options.

TAX REPORTS

Where to find this in Shopify? Analytics > Reports > Taxes

How do you see what your collected taxes are?

To see what you've collected on taxes, go to the left sidebar in your Shopify dashboard and click on '*Analytics.*' Navigate to 'Reports', and scroll to 'Taxes.'

[1.7.25]

Here you can see taxes by channel and which taxes have been filed or not.

DUTIES AND IMPORT TAXES

Your customers might be charged additional duties and taxes if you ship internationally.

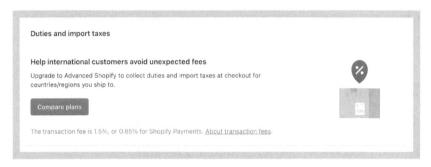

[1.7.24]

Pro Tip: As I suggested, start in your local country before selling across borders. It can become very complicated very fast. Once familiar with your local region or country, add more markets to your Shopify store.

NOTE: *Shopify 'Markets' will be covered in book 3 - Optimize Your Shopify Store. Book 1 is only setting up the basics for your Shopify store.*

HOW TAX IS CHARGED

Manage how taxes are charged and managed in your store. If you are not sure which options to choose, research, and confirm with a local tax consultant or office.

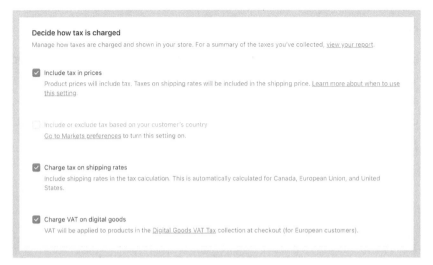

[1.7.20]

Here are you choices:

- **Include tax in price:** *This is common in an international store. The USA norm is not to include tax and show taxes paid on the checkout page for each customer to review.*

- **Include or exclude tax based on your customer's country:** *Your customer's local tax rate will be used for calculations. This option will be not available unless you activate it in Markets preferences.*

- **Charge tax on shipping rate:** *Some states require tax on shipping rates, while some don't. You can include shipping rates in the tax calculation. It is automatically calculated for Canada, European Union, and the United States. Go to your official state or local government website to see what is required.*

- **Charge VAT on digital goods:** *If you are selling digital goods, you need to find out from your local state or government if you need to pay taxes. European customers pay VAT on digital goods sold. If you check this option, digital products will have VAT applied at checkout for European customers. You need to find out more about your EU tax obligation if you are a USA or EU store.*

EUROPEAN UNION VAT

Before setting up EU taxes in Shopify, you must determine whether you should charge taxes. If you're unsure, consult with local tax authorities or a tax professional. Typically, if you intend to sell to countries in the EU, you need to register with the tax authorities in your own country to charge VAT.

Taxes and duties

Manage sales tax collection ℹ️

If you haven't already, create a shipping zone in the region(s) you're liable in. Then, find the region in this list and select it to manage its tax settings. If you're unsure about where you're liable, check with a tax professional.

Country/region	Collecting
🇪🇺 European Union	—
🌐 Rest of World	—

[1.7.28]

Shopify says: "*As of July 1, 2021, distance selling thresholds for individual countries no longer apply. Instead, a single distance selling threshold applies to the entire EU.*

For customers in your home country, your local VAT rate is charged. For customers in EU countries outside your own, the rate is determined by whether you exceed the registration threshold.

If your combined sales to all other EU member countries are less than 10,000 EUR in total, then you can charge your home country's VAT rate in other EU countries and remit VAT to your home country's government. If you choose to charge your home country's VAT rate for all EU sales, then you might need to apply for the micro-business exemption with your local tax authority. If you're not sure whether you need to apply, then consult with your local tax authority or a tax professional.

If your combined sales to all other EU member countries are equal to or greater than 10,000 EUR in total, then you charge the VAT rate in your customer's location for all sales to other countries."

NOTE: Please check this with your local government.

A new One-Stop Shop scheme (OSS) is available as of July 1, 2021. The OSS scheme allows merchants to collect and remit VAT for sales in all EU member countries rather than registering for each member country individually.

Currently, if you're located outside of the EU and you sell to customers within the EU, you aren't required to collect VAT on orders equal to or less than 150 EUR and orders greater than 150 EUR have import VAT and duties applied.

You aren't required to collect VAT regardless of the order amounts. Using IOSS, you can choose to collect VAT on orders equal to or less than 150 EUR at checkout so that your customers don't pay taxes upon delivery.

> Pro Tip: If you are unsure about anything, consult a tax expert.

NOTE: Information for set up of international markets & taxes will in Shopify Made Easy book 3 (2023).

TAX-EXEMPT CUSTOMERS

You can set a customer on your Shopify dashboard Customers' page to be fully tax-exempt.

[1.7.26]

Tax-exempt customers are not charged any tax when they complete checkout. These customers must check out using the same email address on their customer accounts.

Uncheck the tax collection choice. You will need to identify and uncheck each customer individually.

[1.7.27]

RESOURCES:

Research for taxes:

https://www.globalvatcompliance.com/globalvatnews/faqs/what-is-the-difference-between-vat-and-gst/

https://tax.thomsonreuters.com/blog/what-is-the-difference-between-sales-tax-and-vat/

Review the following table to determine which tax service is best for your needs:

https://help.shopify.com/en/manual/taxes/us/choose-tax-service

EU & UK Tax Reference list:

https://help.shopify.com/en/manual/taxes/eu/eu-tax-reference

OSS - All You Need to Know About The Import One-Stop Shop (IOSS):

https://taxation-customs.ec.europa.eu/ioss_en

CHAPTER 9
NOTIFICATIONS

**WHERE *to find this in Shopify? Settings > Notifications*

Notifications will be automatically sent to your customers as soon as an order is placed, fulfilled, shipped, or refunded, an account is registered in Shopify, and a few more options.

What to Expect in This Chapter:

- *Customer Notifications*
- *Customize Email Templates*

CUSTOMER NOTIFICATIONS

You might not need all the notification emails that are in the default Shopify notifications, but the emails are set up for you in Shopify to cover most situations for an online store.

The titles of each email notification indicates the content to your customers and to you or the person you select to process your orders.

CUSTOMIZE EMAIL TEMPLATES

Here are some instructions to add your logo and colors.

[1.9.1]

Step 1. Customize

You can customize your emails with your logo and brand colors. Shopify adds the default blue color for the button and your business name.

[1.9.2]

The business name in 'Store Details' is transferred automatically into the notifications as your header.

[1.9.3]

Once you add your logo and your brand colors, these will be reflected automatically in all your notification emails to your customers.

Step 2. Add your logo and brand colors

Add your logo and your brand colors. Upload your logo from your file on your computer. You can control the width of your logo but don't make it too big. The most important aspect in your notification is your message, not your logo.

Add your accent color, which you added to your store in 'Customize' your theme.

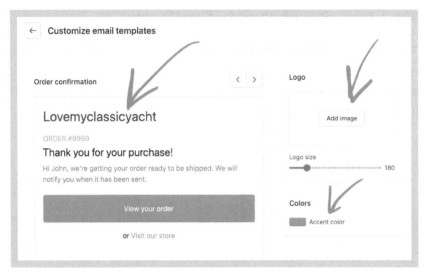

[1.9.2]

The following image is an example of a logo and text, and brand colors. (I know you cannot see the color in the image but if you add the colors etc you will see what I mean.)

[1.9.5]

Next, let's look at the different notifications in Shopify.

Step 3. Personalize email notifications

You can customize the language for each email. The default text is standard in most eCommerce notifications. To change the message in your notifications, the view of the email content in the next image is a snippet of coding.

> Pro Tip: Unless you are familiar with coding, I suggest asking a Shopify expert for help.

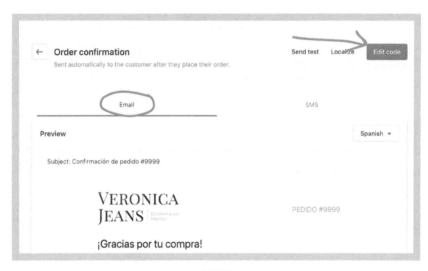

[1.9.7]

As you see in the following image, I have changed the message in my order notification.

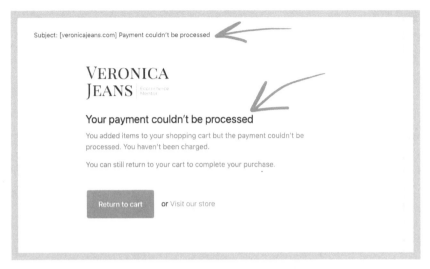

[1.9.6]

ADDING YOUR SIGNATURE

If you want to add your signature to your email, as I have done, here is how you do it.

NOTE: The following steps must be implemented for each notification template separately.

Step 1. Create your signature

Create an image with your signature in software for image creation like Canva.com or Adobe Photoshop. I like to create large images so I can manipulate them and the image does not pixelate. My signature image is 500 px x 129 px (px is pixels).

Step 2. Upload your signature

Open a 'Page' from Shopify's left side of the dashboard. Upload your image with the image icon in the editor. Add the size (recommend 260px) of your image in the details section for the image.

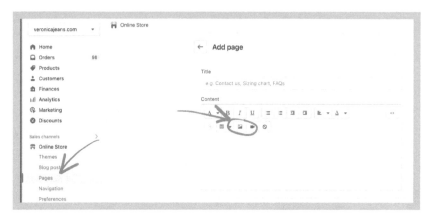

[1.9.9]

Step 3. Open the editor

Once that is done, open the editor to view the code. Click on the chevron icon.

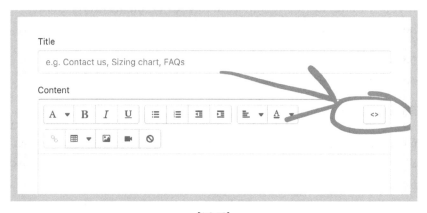

[1.9.10]

Step 4. Add your signature to notifications

Copy the HTML and add the HTML to your notification emails.

Content

```
<div style="text-align: left;"><img
src="https://cdn.shopify.com/s/files/1/1129/4304/files/Signature_Veron
ica_Jeans_Logo_Dark_160x160.png?v=1669988935" alt="Veronica Jeans
Shopify Queen and Bestselling Author" style="float: none;" /></div>
```

[1.9.11]

The following image is an example of my notifications code.

```
606  I will be sending more emails for more information and resources.
607  <br>
608  THANKS a million...<br>
609  Cheers<p>
610              <div style="text-align: left;"><img
     src="https://cdn.shopify.com/s/files/1/1129/4304/files/Signature_Veronica_Jeans_Logo_Dar
     k_160x160.png?v=1669988935" alt="Veronica Jeans Shopify Queen and Bestselling Author"
     style="float: none;" /></div>
611
612              <p class="disclaimer__subtext">If you have any questions or concerns,
     don't hesitate to contact us at any time at <a href="mailto:{{ shop.email }}">{{
     shop.email }}</a></p>
613              </td>
614          </tr>
```

[1.9.12]

You should add your signature, company information or a message to all the notification emails.

> Pro Tip: Add your company information or a message to the email notification to be different! Look at what Donna from the Missing Piece Puzzle added to her email. Including her link to her Facebook page.

[1.9.13]

MOBILE TEXT MESSAGES

When your customers add their mobile number to the checkout, they get their notification via SMS if you have activated the option in your 'Checkout' settings.

Marketing consent
Let customers subscribe to marketing emails and SMS texts at checkout. Learn more about collecting customer marketing consent ⬀ .

Email marketing
☑ Show an option to subscribe at checkout
☑ Preselect the option

SMS marketing
☐ Show an option to subscribe at checkout

[1.9.20]

You **cannot change the text in the SMS** in the 'Notifications' setting. To change the text, add the SMS app to change the notification message.

> Pro Tip: I would leave it as it is because you cannot add too much text to an SMS notification. There are only a certain number of characters allowed.

ABANDON CART EMAIL NOTIFICATION

Your abandoned cart email will be sent according to your schedule in the 'Checkout' settings. You can add your own language or more information in the notification section.

Only one abandoned checkout email is sent according to what you have indicated in the 'Checkout' settings. If you want a series of automated emails for your abandoned cart, you need to use an email provider like Omnisend, MailChimp, Klaviyo, etc.

ORDER NOTIFICATIONS

Here are all the notifications sent when an order is activated:

- *Order confirmation: Sent automatically to the customer after they place their order.*
- *Order edited: Sent to the customer after their order is edited (if you select this option).*
- *Order invoice: Sent to the customer when the order has an outstanding balance.*
- *Order canceled: Sent automatically to the customer if their order is cancelled (if you select this option).*
- *Order refund: Sent automatically to the customer if their order is refunded (if you select this option).*
- *Draft order invoice: Sent to the customer when a draft order invoice is created. You can edit this email invoice before you send it.*
- *Abandoned POS checkout: Sent to the customer when you email their cart from POS. Includes a link to buy online.*
- *Abandoned checkout: Sent to the customer if they leave checkout before they buy the items in their cart. Configure options in 'Checkout settings.'*
- *POS and mobile receipt: Sent to the customer after they complete an in-person order and want to be emailed a receipt.*

- *POS exchange receipt:* Sent to the customer after they complete an exchange in person and want to be emailed a receipt.
- *POS exchange V2 receipt:* Sent to the customer after they complete an exchange V2 in person and want to be emailed a receipt.
- *Gift card created:* Sent automatically to the customer when you issue or fulfill a gift card.
- *Payment error:* Sent automatically to the customer if their payment can't be processed during checkout.
- *Pending payment error:* Sent automatically to the customer if their pending payment can't be processed after checking out.
- *Pending payment success:* Sent automatically to the customer when their pending payment is successfully processed after checking out.

Learn more about payment errors, pending payment errors, and success. See the link in the resources section of this chapter.

SHIPPING NOTIFICATIONS

As in the 'Orders' section, the 'Shipping' section is set up for how your notifications will be sent to your customers.

Shipping	
Fulfillment request	Sent automatically to a third-party fulfillment service provider when order items are fulfilled.
Shipping confirmation	Sent automatically to the customer when their order is fulfilled (if you select this option).
Shipping update	Sent automatically to the customer if their fulfilled order's tracking number is updated (if you select this option).
Out for delivery	☑ Sent to the customer automatically after orders with tracking information are out for delivery.
Delivered	☑ Sent to the customer automatically after orders with tracking information are delivered.

[1.9.14]

Here are all the notifications sent when an order is shipped:

- **Fulfillment request:** *Sent automatically to a third-party fulfillment service provider when order items are fulfilled. Your fulfillment service in Settings > Shipping & Delivery - if you have chosen this service, this notification will be activated once you receive an order,*
- **Shipping information:** *Sent automatically to the customer when their order is fulfilled (if you select this option). Shipping confirmation to your customer, which you can select the 'Delivery' section in the same notifications page.*
- **Shipping update:** *Sent automatically to the customer if their fulfilled order's tracking number is updated (if you select this option). A shipping update is sent to your customer once you have added your tracking number to the orders.*
- **Out for delivery:** *Sent to the customer automatically after orders with tracking information are out for delivery. if you have added a tracking number, this notification will be sent out automatically to your customers.*
- **Delivered:** *Sent to the customer automatically after orders with tracking information are delivered - as soon as the product has been delivered, your customer will be automatically notified.*

The delivery notifications are the optional emails you can send to your customers. It is a good idea to choose these options. Your customers will always like to know where their package is. Amazon has trained all its customers to expect this service. So, don't miss this important step in your customer service strategy.

LOCAL DELIVERY NOTIFICATIONS

If you activate local delivery in 'Shipping and Delivery' setting, check the boxes in this option. As I have noted before, give your customers as many notifications as possible to make them trust you.

Here are all the notifications sent for local deliveries:

- **Out for deliver:** *Sent to the customer when their local order is out for delivery.*
- **Delivered:** *Sent to the customer when their local order is delivered.*
- **Missed delivery:** *Sent to the customer when they miss a local delivery.*

Local delivery

Out for delivery	☑ Sent to the customer when their local order is out for delivery.
Delivered	☑ Sent to the customer when their local order is delivered.
Missed delivery	☑ Sent to the customer when they miss a local delivery.

[1.9.15]

LOCAL PICKUP

If you activate local pickup in 'Shipping and Delivery' settings, these automatic email notifications will be sent out with your customer's orders.

Here are all the notifications sent for local pickup:

- **Ready for pickup:** *Sent to the customer manually through Point of Sale or admin. Lets the customer know their order is ready to be picked up. The message in this notification is the one you added in the 'Shipping and Delivery' setting.*
- **Picked up:** *Sent to the customer when the order is marked as picked up. This is an important notification because it verifies the*

pickup so that there is not come back from the customer that the
package was not picked up.

[1.9.16]

You can preview any notification as see what your message looks
like as in the following image.

VERONICA
JEANS Ecommerce
Mentor

ORDER #9999

Your order is ready for pickup
Bring your confirmation email when you come to collect your order.

Pickup location
Example Shop
34 Example Street
Next to example
Ottawa Ontario K1N5T5
Open map →

View your order   **or** Visit our store

[1.9.17]

CUSTOMER RELATIONSHIP NOTIFICATIONS

These notification emails are utilized when your customer creates
an account or a notification from your customer's order is activated
and sent automatically.

Here are all the notifications sent to maintain a good relationship with your customers:

Customer account invite: Sent to the customer with account activation instructions. You can edit this email before you send it.

- *Customer account welcome: Sent automatically to the customer when they complete their account activation.*
- *Customer account password reset: Sent automatically to the customer when they ask to reset their account password.*
- *Customer payment method update request: Sent to the customer when they ask to update their stored payment method.*
- *B2B access email: (only Shopify+ plan) Sent to a customer when they are added to a company.*
- *Contact customer: Sent to the customer when you contact them from the orders or customers page. You can edit this email before you send it.*

Customer	
Customer account invite	Sent to the customer with account activation instructions. You can edit this email before you send it.
Customer account welcome	Sent automatically to the customer when they complete their account activation.
Customer account password reset	Sent automatically to the customer when they ask to reset their accounts password.
Customer payment method update request	Sent to the customer when they ask to update their stored payment method.
Contact customer	Sent to the customer when you contact them from the orders or customers page. You can edit this email before you send it.

[1.9.18]

Email Marketing

In the 'Checkout' section, you can create an automatic consent for your customer for email marketing. If you have a business in Europe, the UK, etc., where GDPR (General Data Protection Regulation) is effective, you will not check this option.

As a USA business owner, you have the option, but some consequences also involve GDPR. This will probably be affected in the USA in the future, but there have been no regulations set up yet. Check the resources at the end of this chapter for more information.

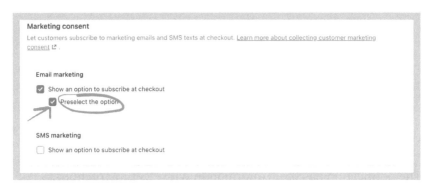

[1.9.19]

RETURN NOTIFICATIONS

In your orders in the Shopify dashboard, you can return and refund your customers per order. Your return instruction notification email will be sent out automatically when you activate a return for a customer order.

- *Return instructions with label/tracking: Sent to the customer when you first create a return that contains a return label or tracking information.*
- *Return requested: Sent automatically to the customer after they have requested a return.*
- *Return approved: Sent to the customer when you approve a requested return.*

- **Return declined:** *Sent to the customer when you decline a requested return.*
- **Return label only:** *Sent to the customer when you add a return label after creating the initial return.*

Returns

Return instructions with label/tracking	Sent to the customer when you first create a return that contains a return label or tracking information.
Return requested	Sent automatically to the customer after they have requested a return.
Return approved	Sent to the customer when you approve a requested return.
Return declined	Sent to the customer when you decline a requested return.
Return label only	Sent to the customer when you add a return label after creating the initial return.

[1.9.23]

The notification has basic information with clear instructions.

Once you have generated a return shipping label, the return label instructions will be sent out automatically with the return instruction notification. The customer can print out the shipping label.

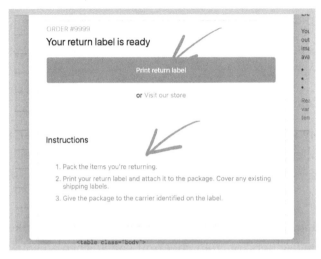

[1.9.24]

Marketing Notifications

In this section, you control, manage and track email marketing consent options.

Step 1. Double Opt-In

To comply with any regulation, you can require your customer to confirm their subscription. If you check these options, you get explicit consent from customers to send them email and SMS marketing.

This option allows customers to agree first to receive marketing emails (newsletters) on your checkout pages. Then an email will be sent to the customer's email address to verify they signed up for email marketing.

Customers who sign up will receive a confirmation message to validate their subscription. Previous subscribers will not be affected.

You can control which notification is required for double opt-in:

Email subscription or SMS subscription

[1.9.22]

Remember, customers sign up for email marketing when they check out of your store. For customers to be able to sign up for email newsletters, you need to initiate this in '*Settings*' and '*Checkout*' under '*Marketing options.*'

You must check the 'To receive shipping updates' option so your customer can sign up for marketing emails (newsletters).

Step 2. Shopify email open tracking

Email tracking notifies you when any email you sent has been opened or clicked. Email tracking software (in this case Shopify) places an invisible image pixel in your emails that can detect the exact time and date a recipient has opened an email.

It is always a good idea to track if customers are opening their emails. Shopify now offers email marketing and automation. You can also use a third-party provider for your email marketing, but then the Shopify tracking will not be activated.

Shopify offers these options:

- *Optimize open tracking: Choose this option to balance tracking open email rates with maintaining your sender reputation.*
- *Ask for consent: By default, email opens will not be tracked. However, subscribers can opt-in to tracking through the footer of your emails. Your open rate will be reported based on subscribers who opt in, combined with overall engagement.*
- *Do not track: Your email open rate will not be reported. However, you will still be able to see other metrics, such as the number of clicks from subscribers in your emails.*
- *Tracks all email opens: See how many subscribers open your emails. This will provide the most accurate reporting on open behavior.*

Shopify Email open tracking

Open tracking allows you to see how many emails are opened.

○ Optimize open tracking (recommended)
Choose this option to balance tracking email open rates with maintaining your sender reputation.

○ Ask for consent
By default, email opens will not be tracked. Subscribers will be able to opt-in to tracking through the footer of your emails. Your open rate will be reported based on subscribers who opt-in, combined with overall engagement.

○ Do not track
Your email open rate will not be reported. You will still be able to see other metrics, such as the number of clicks from subscribers in your emails.

◉ Tracks all email opens
See how many subscribers open your emails. This will provide the most accurate reporting into open behavior.

[1.9.25]

Here are some benefits for tracking all email opens:

- *It is easy to see how many and who opened the emails. This gives you a good indicator how successful the message is so you can improve your messages. It is good to test variations of email messages.*
- *Where each person clicked and what their interest is so you can show them similar products or information.*
- *It shows if you have bounced emails, which either means they could not be delivered, which could indicate no email for your customer, or the wrong email address. This is an opportunity to weed these email addresses out of your list.*
- *In Shopify, tracking shows you the conversion rate with each email campaign.*

There is always room to improve in all marketing efforts.

Performance			
Opened >	Clicked >	Reported as spam >	Unsubscribed >
1,312 46.2% open rate	**34** 1.2% click rate	**4**	**7**
Delivered >	Bounced >		
2,837	**8**		

[1.9.26]

Step 3. How to find your marketing customers

Where to find this in Shopify? Settings > Customers

You will find your customers that have opted-in for email marketing subscriptions in 'Customers' and 'Accepts Marketing'. No email newsletters or other email marketing will be allowed to be sent to your customers if they do not agree to this option.

[1.9.27]

STAFF ORDER NOTIFICATIONS

When an order is placed in your store, the email notifications are sent to you, your staff, and your team. For example, the email lets you know what is in the order, who it is from, etc.

There are several ways to get notified by your Shopify store when a product has been purchased.

- *Email notification*
- *Desktop notification*
- *SMS*

There are different ways to add a contact email address.

- *You can add one of your staff members who is already added to your Shopify 'Users & Permissions' setting. The email address will be automatically allocated.*
- *You can add a new address for managing orders.*

If you want to receive the order notifications by SMS, download the Shopify App. With the App, you can access your whole store on your mobile.

Staff order notifications

Choose how you want to be notified ⬈ when a new order comes in or add other recipients. You can also subscribe to the RSS feed ⬈ for this store's orders.

Add recipient

[1.9.28]

You can specify from which location they will be notified.

Add an order notification   ✕

Notification method

Email address ⇕

Location

All ⇕

Email address

To get notifications on your phone, download the Shopify Mobile app .

Cancel   Add an order notification

[1.9.29]

You can view who and where the order notifications are going and control the access here.

[1.9.30]

Here are the steps to add an SMS for your staff notifications:

Step 1. Add Recipient

In the Shopify App (on your mobile), log into your Shopify store. In the bottom left corner, click on 'Store' (left image) and, then, 'Settings' (second image below). Navigate to 'Notifications' to add the team member to your staff notifications (third image below).

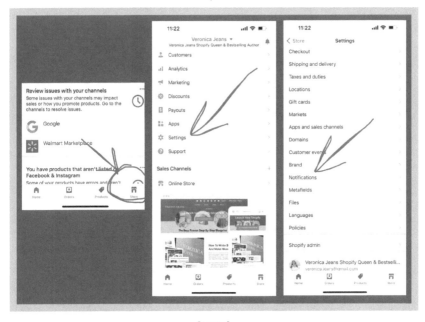

[1.9.31]

Pro Tip: If your customers or staff aren't receiving email notifications, have them check their spam or junk folder. This is an excellent opportunity to connect with your customers to give them great support. Then, email them to check if they have received the order notification.

Step 2. Templates

You can add or change the information in this email notification. However, only you, your staff, and your team will see this email. This notification will show the complete order, the payment processing method, the shipping method the customer chose, and the customer's information.

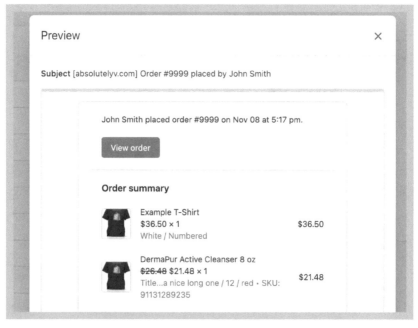

[1.9.32]

Step 3. Draft Order

Draft orders are a great tool in your Shopify store.

Draft orders

New draft order   ☑ Sent to store owner when a customer submits an order for review.

[1.9.34]

Here are some reasons why you would create a draft order:

- *When you need to create an order on behalf of a customer. You add the customer details and products and then send an invoice, collect a payment, or set payment terms.*
- *When the order is paid for or when you set payment terms, the draft order converts to an order and is listed on your 'Orders' setting.*
- *You can use draft orders to sell directly to consumers or to sell to other businesses.*
- *You can create an order to accept payment for orders placed over the phone, in person, or by email.*
- *Send an invoice to a customer and they can pay with a secure link in the invoice.*
- *Sell products at a discount or wholesale rates.*
- *Take pre-orders.*
- *Use custom items to represent additional costs or products that aren't displayed in your inventory.*

Great example: I had to include a liftgate charge with the shipping cost for one of my clients. I created a draft order and sent him the invoice.

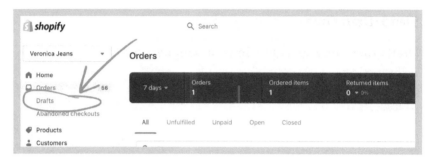

[1.9.35]

RESOURCES:

Here is a link to my TOOLS page: **https://veronicajeans.online/ resources**

Learn more about payment errors, pending payment errors, and success. Check Chapter 4 'Integrating Payments in Shopify.'

CHAPTER 10

FILES, LANGUAGE & POLICIES

IN THIS CHAPTER I have combined three sections from the 'Settings' option because they are easy and quick.

What to Expect in This Chapter:

- *Files*
- *Language*
- *Policies*
- *Contact information*

FILES

Where to find this in Shopify? Content > Files

Most images, videos, or files are stored in the '*Files*' setting. When you upload files in the approved format in your Theme, collections, products, blog, pages, etc., the files will be automatically added in '*Files.*'

Files on the '*Files*' setting can include the following:

- *Images and videos used in your theme, blog posts, and pages.*
- *Images and videos used in your product and collection descriptions.*
- *Files and videos that you want to make available for customers to download.*
- *Images and files connected to 'Metafields.'*
- *PDFs (Portable Document Format - Adobe Acrobat) for ebooks, any printed material, size charts, etc.*

File Size Requirements

File size requirements for images:

Image file requirements	
Attribute	**Requirement**
File size	Maximum of 20 MB (megabytes)
Resolution	Maximum of 20 MP (megapixels)
Aspect ratio	Between 100:1 and 1:100
File formats	JPEG, PNG, WEBP, HEIC, and GIF

[1.10.1]

File size requirements for videos:

Video file requirements	
Attribute	**Requirement**
File size	Maximum of 1 GB (gigabyte)
Resolution	Maximum resolution of 4K
Video length	Maximum video length of 10 minutes
File formats	MOV and MP4

[1.10.2]

> Pro Tip: If you have text or spreadsheet documents, you need to create a PDF format before uploading the documents to Shopify.

This is not the right option if you need to upload files for products. You will find the import and export option in the 'Products' setting.

If you want to import blogs, pages, collections, and products, the best way is with an App - I suggest using Matrixify.

How to Use & Upload Pdfs in Your Store

You can only upload a PDF in 'Files.' The PDF is stored on the Shopify server and can now be added to any link in the editor on the appropriate page in your store.

Step 1. Upload your PDFs

Upload the PDF to '*Files*.' Click on the chain icon to copy the link. Use it in your pages/product description or wherever you need the information. The customer can then navigate directly to the document.

[1.10.3]

Step 2. Create links to the file

The image below is an example of different links you can create. Add it to a text or phrase or image. Highlight the text and click on the chain-link symbol at the top of your editor. This opens the next view to add your information.

[1.10.3]

Paste the link/URL address from Step 1 into the *'Link to'* box.

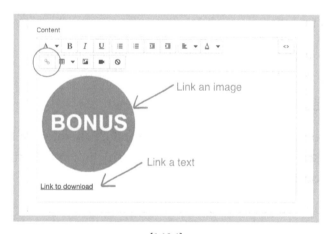

[1.10.4]

Step 3. Choose the open this link option

For '*Open this link in*' - choose one of the options. Open the page in the '*same window*' or a '*new window.*' A '*new window*' opens up another tab in the browser for your visitor.

Step 4. Add a link title

Add a '*link title*' - this is a description or explanation of your image. This is what we call an '*Alt tag* or *alt text*' this is an important step for SEO (Search engine optimization) for your website.

LANGUAGE

**Where to find this in Shopify? Settings > Languages

We like to think that everybody is comfortable shopping in English. But people like shopping in their own language. Shopify makes it possible.

NOTE: *Translating your store to different languages is not an easy proposition. If you are comfortable with Google Translate, then you are okay. It is not easy to translate Spanish, for instance, to Mexico, Spain, and other Spanish countries. Each country will have its own variation of the Spanish language. If you decide to go this route, you will need to verify your language in your store.*

Not every Shopify store can translate to a different language. Here are some requirements:

- *Basic Shopify plan or higher*
- *A theme that's compatible with selling in multiple languages.*
- *A theme that has a language selector.*
- *Translate & Adapt Shopify or third-party translation app.*

> Pro Tip: Language translation does not work well with dialects. If you sell to a localized dialect, you will have to manually adapt and change the language.

Step 1. Add a language

The main language will be the default in your Shopify store. You can add more languages depending on your Shopify plan.

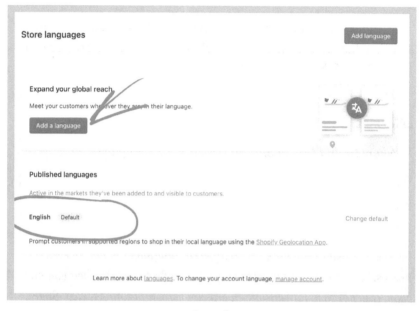

[1.10.5]

Once you decide to add a new language, the '*Adapt & Translate*' app from Shopify will be added automatically.

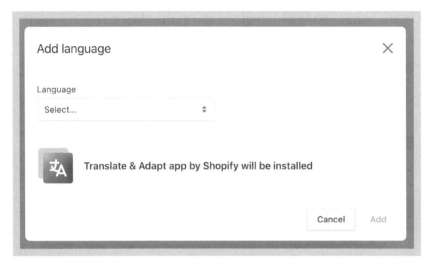

[1.10.5b]

In the following image, you can see what it would look like in your store if you activated different languages. The view is shown and can be customized in *'Geo Location'* app (which is a fee Shopify app when you activate Geo locations).

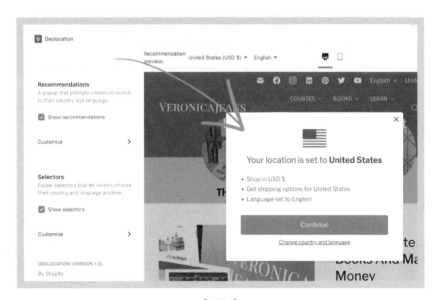

[1.10.6]

Once you have added a language, this is the view you will have in your '*Language*' setting.

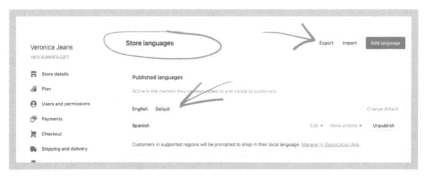

[1.10.5a]

Step 2. Change default language

You can change your default language to any language available. Some page might be translatable.

[1.10.12]

Step 3. Add & translate more languages.

You will be pushed to the 'Translate & Adapt' app when you add or publish more languages.

Auto Translate: You're about to use automatic translation for Spanish. This will be the first of your 2 free languages. After Spanish, you can auto-translate into 1 more language. The translations will not be visible to your customers until you publish them. Automatically translate your store content using translation software powered by Google Translate.

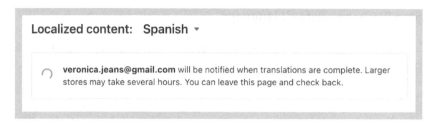

[1.10.7]

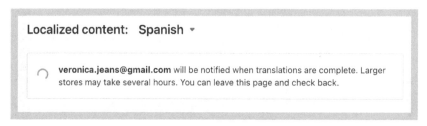

[1.10.8]

Here are the benefits of the Translate & Adapt App in Shopify:

- *Localize everywhere: Localize right from where you create content across Shopify. Access the editor by finding Localize under More actions for any resources like products or collections and in your Online Store sections. You can also access the editor by selecting a resource from the app home page.*
- *Side-by-side editor: Translate your content into other languages. When adding new languages to your store, you'll be able to easily add, edit and review translations for each language with the editor.*
- *Store content by market: Customize your content for different markets. Account for spelling, vocabulary, and messaging variations to provide a shopping experience tailored for different markets. When viewing translations, switch between markets to add a customized version.*
- *Auto-translate: Automatically translate your store. Use the free automatic translation option for up to 2 languages to quickly translate your store content, and manually translate up to 20*

languages. Whenever you add any new content in your default language, remember to run automatic translation again, or manually add new translations.

- ***Edit and review:*** *Everything in one place. Move between all of your store's translatable and customizable content. Polish up and publish for your customers, wherever they are.*

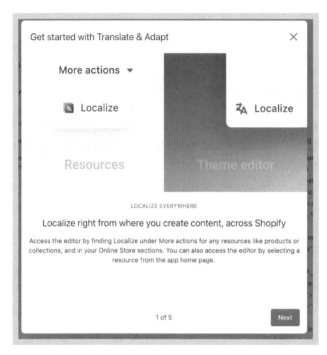

[3.11.1]

Step 4. Edit Language

**Where to find this in Shopify? Settings > Apps

Editing the language in Shopify will be done in the Translate & Adapt app. Click on 'Edit' in any section you need and both languages will appear - the original and the translation.

[3.11.2a]

- **All supported markets:** *You can change each market in the dropdown 'All supported markets' and change it to any market (country).*
- **Language:** *Choose the language you want to edit. Side-by-side editor - notification is in the code view. Code remains in English but the language changes to the language chosen.*
- **Notifications or the selection** *you chose to edit i.e. 'Collections', 'Products' etc. The specific section will open for editing. You can change your selection in the left sidebar.*
- **Auto-translate:** *If you have not auto-translated your language yet, click the 'Auto-translate' button and confirm to auto-translate. This action will automatically translate all empty and outdated fields into Spanish. This will not replace any manual translations you have added.*
- **View Store:** *You can view any page or the complete store once you click on this button.*

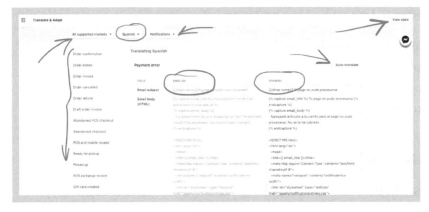

[3.11.2b]

Once you are in this Shopify setting you will able to see what portions are translated or not.

Step 5. Add more languages to different markets.

If you are changing the language, you can add the language to a specific market. As you see in the following image, I have added Spanish to Mexico.

[1.10.13]

Step 6. Import and export languages.

Whenever translations don't exist, your online store shows content in your primary language. You can translate the content of your online store by adding your own translation using a CSV file, or by using a third-party app.

After translating the store, customers can browse your store, checkout, and receive notifications in their local language.

See in the following image how to import your language.

Check the box if you want to overwrite the existing language.

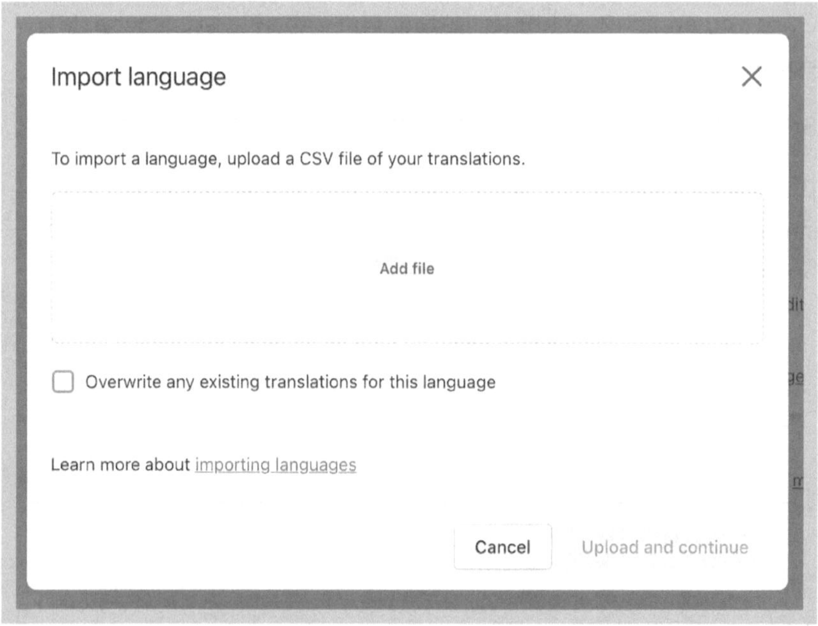

Import language   ✕

To import a language, upload a CSV file of your translations.

Add file

☐ Overwrite any existing translations for this language

Learn more about importing languages

Cancel   Upload and continue

[1.10.10]

I like to check all the data that I have in my store. So downloading your language to check it is a great idea.

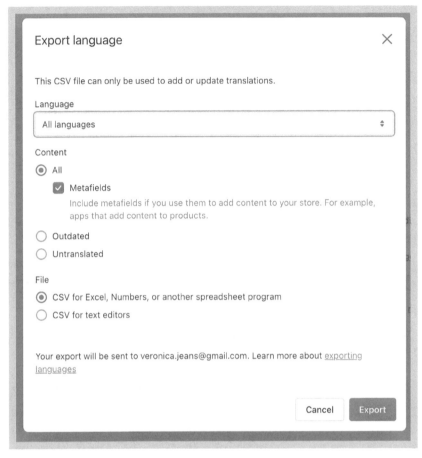

Export language   ✕

This CSV file can only be used to add or update translations.

Language

| All languages | ⇕ |

Content

◉ All

☑ Metafields
    Include metafields if you use them to add content to your store. For example,
    apps that add content to products.

◯ Outdated

◯ Untranslated

File

◉ CSV for Excel, Numbers, or another spreadsheet program

◯ CSV for text editors

Your export will be sent to veronica.jeans@gmail.com. Learn more about exporting
languages

                                        Cancel   Export

[1.10.11]

Step 7. Language selectors

***Where to find this in Shopify? Settings > Online Store > Themes
> Customize***

If you do not have a second language selected, then the option will
not be shown in Themes.

[1.10.23]

In your Theme, click on the 'Header' section and the options will either appear on the right sidebar, as shown in image 1.10.24 or the left sidebar as a shown in image 1.10.25, depending on your theme or view.

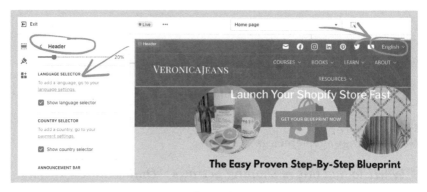

[1.10.24]

[1.10.25]

This will give your store visitor the option to read the information in their own language.

POLICIES

**Where to find this in Shopify? Settings >Legal*

[1.10.14]

Why do you need legal policies in your eCommerce store?

Policies are a necessity for your eCommerce business. You need legal documentation for your eCommerce store to protect your business because you are collecting personal data like names, email addresses, IP addresses, session activity, and payment details, to name a few.

Shopify has legal templates ready to use within the dashboard, but they will have to be edited to suit your requirements. Not every online store has the same legal issues or needs protection. It is always better to check your information with your own legal counsel.

Types of legal documentation in Shopify:

- *Refund Policy*
- *Privacy Policy*
- *Terms of Service*
- *Shipping Policy*
- *Contact Information*

An explanation for each of the legal pages you will add to your online store.

REFUND POLICY

This is an essential part of the legal documentation for any retail business to provide to its customers. This definitely can convince a customer to trust your store, which could be vital to closing the sale.

A refund policy is exactly as it sounds - a policy that dictates the terms of any refunds or returns, which may be offered by the website or eCommerce store.

Before you make a purchase, you may decide to review the refund policy of a given website or store to make sure you are comfortable with the terms. For instance, if a site says that "all sales are final" and no refunds will be issued, you may think twice about placing an order. On the other hand, if another business offers a "60- day, no questions asked" refund, you will be more comfortable with spending your money on their site.

Privacy Policy

In an eCommerce store, we collect personal data from our customers. It would help if you let your customers know how you handle their personal data, protect their data, and control their own data. If your customer requests their data from you, you are legally bound to provide it for them, and once you provide their data to the customer, you are legally bound not to keep the data in-house.

A well-written Privacy Policy protects you from unnecessary risks or legal issues that could arise from conflicts with customers over the management of their personal data. It also protects you from legal issues with regulators and third parties requiring you to have a Privacy Policy.

If you are dealing with California online customers, you must have all the CalOPPA (California Online Privacy Protection Act of 2003) information in your privacy policy.

If you have EU customers, you need to know more about GDPR (General Data Protection Regulation), which went into effect in May 2018. These regulations create a higher level of privacy protection for any EU resident. So just because you think you do not sell in the EU, you might have EU residents shopping online while they are in the USA.

Whatever you do, always try to cover every eventuality. This might develop as you grow your business, but always keep in mind to add more information as new rules and regulations are required. Shopify provides ample time to implement these issues when they occur.

Terms Of Service

This policy sets the terms of use for your customers on your website/store. A terms and conditions policy, also known as terms of service or terms of use, is a legal document developed to protect the company. It tells your customers what will be legally required of them if they use your service (including websites and mobile apps). Shopify provides this free for you. This was very comprehensive and adequate for my clients' stores.

Godaddy.com says: *"Terms of Use" (sometimes called "Terms of Service" or "Terms and Conditions") is a way for you to set up rules and regulations for visitors using your business's website. It's also a way to protect your business by limiting liability if a customer were to take you to court. Although there's no legal requirement for defining the terms and conditions for using your website, you might consider creating some for legal protection."*

SHIPPING POLICY

A shipping policy informs your customer of all the information about shipping carriers, time to ship, how they will receive their products and so much more.

It is important to make this as comprehensive as possible to inform your customer but also to protect you.

CONTACT INFORMATION

Contact information is required on your website if you are selling into the European Union.

CREATE YOUR LEGAL PAGES

Shopify makes it very easy to add legal policies to your store. The default information will be automatically generated for you in the editing area. Check the information to see if you need to change anything. Remember to SAVE.

Step 1. Refund Policy

You must edit this page to reflect your business and store information. The default page only gives you suggestions. A detailed refund policy will be created if you click the 'Create from template' button. Now edit the policy to suit your niche market.

[1.10.14]

Step 2. Privacy Policy

You will not usually have to make as many changes as with the refund policy on this page. I would leave most of this page because it covers most of what you need on a privacy page. Throughout the page, you will be prompted to add more information.

Example - [[INSERT DESCRIPTIONS OF OTHER TYPES OF TRACKING TECHNOLOGIES USED]] or [[INSERT ANY OTHER PAYMENT TYPES ACCEPTED]])

Unless you have more information, delete any information you do not need. A detailed policy is automatically added to the editor if you click the 'Create from template' button. Now read through all the information and add or delete it as needed.

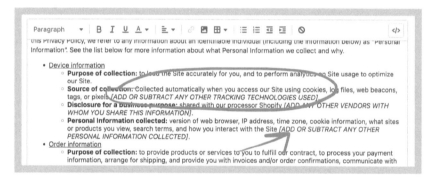

[1.10.16]

Step 3. Terms of Service

The Terms of Service page you can leave as is unless you have legal information you need to add. If you click the 'Create from template' button, detailed policy information is automatically added to the editor.

Terms of service

Paragraph ▾ | B *I* U A ▾ | ≣ ▾ | 🖾 ⊞ ▾ | ≣ ≣ ≣ ≣ | ⃠ </>

OVERVIEW
This website is operated by Namibia Marketplace. Throughout the site, the terms "we", "us" and "our" refer to Namibia Marketplace. Namibia Marketplace offers this website, including all information, tools and Services available from this site to you, the user, conditioned upon your acceptance of all terms, conditions, policies and notices stated here.

By visiting our site and/ or purchasing something from us, you engage in our "Service" and agree to be bound by the following terms and conditions ("Terms of Service", "Terms"), including those additional terms and conditions and policies referenced herein and/or available by hyperlink. These Terms of Service apply to all users of the site, including without limitation users who are browsers, vendors, customers, merchants, and/ or contributors of content.

Please read these Terms of Service carefully before accessing or using our website. By accessing or using any part of the site, you agree to be bound by these Terms of Service. If you do not agree to all the terms and conditions of this agreement, then you may not access the website or use any Services. If these Terms of Service are considered an offer, acceptance is expressly limited to these Terms of Service.

[1.10.17]

Step 4. Shipping Policy

The last page is your Shipping Policy page. There is no '*Create from template*' button. You have to create the shipping information in accordance to your shipping requirements and information. Again, it helps to do research with established brands and other businesses in the same niche market, because they probably have more experience with customer service and problems.

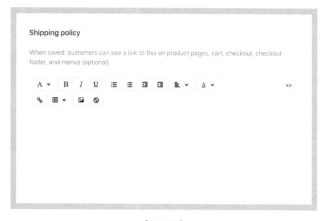

[1.10.18]

You should give your customers as much information as possible. According to your customers' questions, you might have to add more details later if you are a new store. Initially, you can add enough shipping information from your shipping carriers to satisfy your customers.

> Pro Tip: Check out your compatriots /competition and see and see what they have. Or research a random website (larger stores) and see what they have on their Shipping Information. DO NOT COPY.

Try to answer some of the shipping questions and add more information you create yourself on your page in your own words.

Remember, this is about giving your customers information so they can make an informed decision to buy from you.

For instance:

- *How long your shipping time is (check with your shipping carrier) and other pertinent information your customer will need to know what will happen when that package is on the way.*
- *What happens if it gets damaged, or when they get their tracking code, if it goes to the wrong address, etc.*

Don't forget to add your **international shipping policy information**. If you do not ship internationally, you still must let prospective buyers know your policy. For example: *"We do not ship internationally"*.

Step 5. Contact Information

If you have an international store, information about your business must be added to the *'Contact Information'* box.

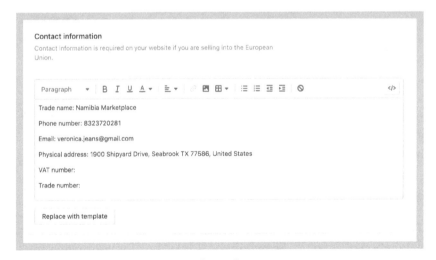

[1.10.20]

If you click the *'Create from template'* button, information will be automatically added. You might need to augment the information.

Step 6. Add a Legal Page to Navigation

Once you have created your legal page, you will add the legal page you created to your navigation.

The 'Navigation' is in the 'Online Store' setting. Once you either change the default menu or add a new menu, add your legal pages to your menus.

[1.10.21]

Usually, the legal and other information your customer will need is in your footer menu (which is located at the bottom of. Your page). In Shopify, the footer menu is named *'Footer'* or *'Quick Links'*, but I suggest you change it to 'Information' or something more descriptive.

You add your link for your legal page on the right side of your navigation dashboard. Search in the 'Links' box for your pages in 'Policies'.

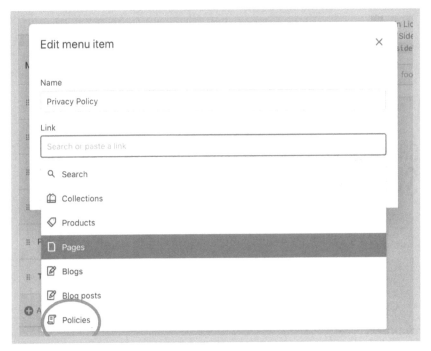

[1.10.22]

Once you have added them to your menu, you need to add the menu to your store.

To be able to add any menus to your online pages, go to 'Online store' and click on 'Customize'. Once you are in the Customize dashboard, you can add the footer. Menus to the 'Footer' setting.

Now you will be able to see your legal pages in your online store.

CHAPTER 11
SHOPIFY POINT OF SALE

**WHERE *to find this in Shopify? Settings > Apps and sales channels*

In this chapter, we will only add the Shopify Point of Sale (POS) app for the online store. We will not cover any technology or hardware options for the POS system. This is for an online store and being able to utilize your store at events, pop-up shops etc.

Responding fast is essential for businesses to compete in fierce competition for customers. Shopify offers a variety of inherent Apps that make it possible to run your business wherever you are.

What to Expect in This Chapter:

- *Set up Point of Sale Apps and Sales Channels*
- *Hardware for the Point of Sale system.*

SET UP POINT OF SALE APPS AND SALES CHANNELS

[1.3.28]

Here are the features of the Shopify POS app:

Process Orders

- *Fulfill, refund, or archive orders for each of your store locations*
- *Print packing slips and shipping labels*
- *Manage tags and notes*
- *Contact customers*
- *Add Timeline comments*
- *Track conversion right from your order details*
- *Create new draft orders and send them to your customers*
- *View fraud analysis*

Manage Products and Collections

- *Add products manually or through bar code scan*
- *Create and update automated or manual collections*
- *Manage product tags and categories*

- *Define product and collection visibility on sales channels*
- *Sync with 3rd party sites to sell on Etsy, Amazon, eBay, and more*

Run Marketing Campaigns

- *Grow sales with a Google Smart Shopping campaign*
- *Create Facebook ads on the go*
- *Track results and get custom recommendations to improve your results over time*
- *Write new content for your blog*

Follow Up with Customers

- *Add and edit customer details*
- *Contact customers*

Create Discounts

- *Create special discounts for holidays and sales*
- *Monitor discount code usage*

Review Store Performance

- *View sales reports by day, week, or month*
- *Compare sales across your online store and other sales channels with a live dashboard*

Sell on More Sales Channels

- *Sell online, in-store and more*
- *Reach your customers wherever you're selling*
- *Sync inventory and orders across each channel*

Extend Your Store's Features with Apps and Themes

- *Access your Shopify apps from orders, products, and customers, or right from the Store tab*
- *Browse our catalog of free themes and change your online store appearance*

Adding shortcuts to Siri for sales, visitors and orders is another cool feature of the App Settings on mobile.

Not all the above-mentioned features are in Shopify POS Lite. The following are only in the Shopify POS Pro app subscription.

- *Automatic discounts*
- *Unlimited POS-only staff*
- *Sales attribution*
- *Exchanges*
- *Save /retrieve cart*
- *Ship to home*
- *Local pickup fulfillment*
- *Local delivery fulfillment*
- *Advanced inventory management with Stocky*
- *Daily sales reports*
- *In-app retail store analytics*

Step 1. Add the POS app

The POS app is in the Shopify App Store. Once you navigate to the online App Store, search for 'Shopify POS' and add the app to your store.

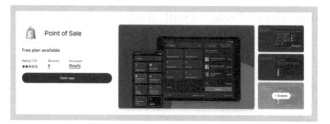

[1.3.33]

Step 2. Approve the POS app

You need to approve the POS app on your mobile phone to be able to load the app on your phone.

[1.3.30]

Step 3. Choose the POS options

You can sell at markets and fairs, pop-ups, and in-person events.

Tell us about your retail business to get started.

Where do you want to sell in person?
Select any that might interest you — it's okay if you change your mind later.

☐ At markets and fairs

☐ At pop-ups

☐ In my own brick and mortar store(s)

Skip   Submit

[1.3.31]

Step 5. Set up your devices

You can set up the POS app on your phone or tablet. Download the app on your chosen device and sign in with the same credentials you have for your store.

Review POS subscriptions for each location

1900 SHIPYARD DR LITE
1900 SHIPYARD DR   ⦿ Lite   ○ Pro
Seabrook Texas 77586
United States

Warehouse LITE
15520 Galveston Road
#205   ⦿ Lite   ○ Pro
Webster Texas 77598
United States

Cancel   Save

[1.3.32]

Step 6. Choose your location

Your location will pop up, so just pick the right one.

Step 7. Allow app permissions

You can change these anytime. If you are doing events in different locations, you will have to activate the location services and WIFI every time you attend the event.

- *Location services: Required to accept card payments.*
- *Local network: Needed to connect hardware via WiFi*
- *Camera: Used to scan barcodes with the device camera*
- *Notifications: Allow for local pickup and delivery notifications*

Step 8. Create PIN

Create a unique four-digit PIN to access the Point-of-Sale app. This PIN can be changed at any time. You can generate a random PIN as well.

Step 9. Your POS is activated.

You can start selling.

Step 10. Choose a subscription plan

Choses a Point-of-Sale App and subscription plan. Here are the different POS plans:

- *POS Lite: Accept casual, in-person payments at markets, fairs, pop-ups, and more, automatically set up when you choose your Shopify subscription plan.*
- *POS Pro: Shopify POS Pro syncs with Shopify to track your orders and inventory across your retail locations, online store, and other active sales channels. This will entail Shopify hardware implementation.*

Pricing	See all pricing options
SHOPIFY POS LITE	SHOPIFY POS PRO
Free	**$89/month**
✓ Included with all Shopify plans.	✓ $89/month per location
✓ Best for selling at pop-ups, markets and fairs.	✓ Try Shopify POS Pro features with a 14-day free trial.
	✓ Best for selling at brick-and-mortar stores.

[1.3.29]

If you want to opt to upgrade, your Shopify subscription plan will be upgraded to the Shopify subscription plan of $79/month.

> Pro Tip: If you do not have the knowledge to add hardware or the technology to connect to the hardware, you will need to get an IT specialist to assist.

Hardware available for the POS system:

- *Tap & Chip Reader*
- *Shopify POS Go*
- *Tap & Chip Bundle*

RESOURCES:

You can buy all the hardware in the Shopify hardware store:

https://hardware.shopify.com/

———

This is it for this section of setting your Shopify store up – now you need to get your products up and brand your Shopify store.

———

WHAT IS NEXT FOR YOUR SHOPIFY STORE?

Shopify Made Easy Book 2 - Build Your Customer Journey - a blueprint for setting up the Themes and Products to build your brand with Shopify is the second installment in a groundbreaking series created by Amazon.com Bestselling author, Veronica Jeans, to take you by the hand and walk you into the world of e-commerce.

Learn how to brand your Shopify store with Step-by-Step guides, lots of screenshots, and tips from a Shopify expert.

Join my newsletters for Shopify & marketing courses, resources, and tools on my website: https://veronicajeans.online/resources.

QR Code for Resources

Please Kindly Review This Book

Thank you for reading Shopify Made Easy Book 1. Reviews are crucial for helping other readers discover new books that help them find their own freedom.

If you want to share the value of reading this book, help other readers know how useful this book was for you. I'd really appreciate it.

Recommending my book to others is also a huge help. Don't hesitate to shout out this book in your favorite social media group to spread the word.

QR code for Review on Amazon

Thank you so much!

AFTERWORD

I hope that you found it helpful and that it has helped you on your journey to becoming an online success.

It's time to pull up your sleeves and get to work. Get started today. Because they never start, many online entrepreneurs will never achieve their goals.

Don't be a dreamer. You have to take action.

It will be challenging to get started and often confusing. This is just part of the process. I always say...baby steps.

Others have done it, so you can too!

My last advice is: "Set your goals and keep striving to reach them."

Don't let anyone or anything discourage you. Keeping your eye on those goals and working toward them is the best way to achieve them. This is how most successful entrepreneurs operate.

Be patient, work hard, and be innovative.

Those are the keys to success.

There is no difference between short-term and long-term goals.

I decided to write the 'eCommerce Success Planner' to help you. I created a planner with checkboxes and ideas to help you achieve your goals in 90-day cycles. Every single day is laid out for you, with more note pages.

If you have any questions, let me know.

hello@veronicaleejeans.com

Best wishes on your journey to financial freedom!

ABOUT THE AUTHOR

Veronica Jeans is an eCommerce business consultant and Shopify expert who has coached entrepreneurs to build and negotiate all the intricacies of running an online store.

She has had extensive experience helping eCommerce businesses grow in the global marketplace - from startups to brick-and-mortar stores that want to start their own online outlet for additional revenue streams. She integrates her extensive knowledge in eCommerce and her international financial and tax expertise to offer up a playbook for generating income online.

Veronica lives on a yacht in Houston, Texas but is originally from Namibia. She lived with her hubby and sons in several countries before landing in Texas and has maintained she has landed in entrepreneur heaven.

Veronica is the author of the publications: 'Shopify Made Easy' book series - Build Your Ecommerce Empire, Brand Your Shopify Store, Optimize Your Shopify Store, Position Your Brand, Position Your Brand, Content Marketing for eCommerce, and Shopify Made Easy - Workbook & Checklist.

facebook.com / veronicajeansqueen

twitter.com / VeronicaJeans

instagram.com / shopify.queen

amazon.com / author / veronicajeans

linkedin.com / in / veronicajeans

youtube.com / @VeronicaJeans

pinterest.com / ecommercequeen

ACKNOWLEDGMENTS

I want to thank everybody from the bottom of my heart to allow me to use our interviews and experiences in my book.

Made in United States
Troutdale, OR
04/06/2024